Basic
GLASS FUSING

All the Skills and Tools You Need to Get Started

Lynn Haunstein

*Photographs by
Alan Wycheck*

STACKPOLE
BOOKS

Published by
STACKPOLE BOOKS
5067 Ritter Road
Mechanicsburg, PA 17055
www.stackpolebooks.com

Printed in the United States

10 9 8 7 6 5 4 3

First edition

Cover design by Tracy Patterson

Library of Congress Cataloging-in-Publication Data

Haunstein, Lynn.
  Basic glass fusing / Lynn Haunstein ; photographs by
Alan Wycheck. — 1st
ed.
       p. cm.
   ISBN 978-0-8117-0988-0
  1. Glass fusing. I. Title.
   TT298.H386 2012
   748.2028—dc23

                                              2012005521

Contents

Introduction

Fusing glass in a kiln is a very exciting process. Flat sheets of glass can become beautiful and functional pieces of art when heated to temperatures that bond the glass together or change its shape.

My first class in fused glass was really intriguing. And really confusing. Firing schedules, special glass for fusing, manually operated kilns—there was so much to learn. Over the years, as that first class was followed by more classes, workshops, and lots of practice, the fusing process became clearer. Automatic kilns took the guesswork out of firing schedules. Manufacturers began offering more fusing glass, and I learned new techniques from experienced fusers. The projects I made became more functional and creative.

The goal of this book is to take the confusion out of fusing and slumping glass. You'll find all the information you need about the specific glass developed for fusing as well as the decorative components you can use to enhance your projects. Kilns and firing schedules are discussed in detail. For those with little or no experience in basic stained glass cutting, I have included a chapter to hone those skills. You will find easy-to-follow directions for numerous fused glass projects that will begin at the most basic level and increase in difficulty.

Once you have mastered the basic skills for fusing and slumping glass, you can use your creative spirit to explore unlimited possibilities in this art form.

I hope this book will simplify the kiln process for you as you learn new techniques in working with glass.

1

Glass for Fusing

Nearly any glass can be fired in the kiln by itself. However, when two or more pieces of glass are fired together, we must respect their rates of expansion when heated, and contraction when cooled. Glass manufacturers test their glass and assign the appropriate number for that expansion and contraction rate. This number is called the Coefficient of Expansion, or COE.

Glass and accent pieces with the same COE number are considered compatible. When fusing a project, you will want to use only compatible glass and components. A fusing project made with glass or components that are not compatible may contain stress. During the firing process, or any time thereafter, a project containing stress may develop cracks and eventually break.

COMPATIBILITY

Manufacturers offer fusing glass in a variety of COE numbers; 104, 96, 90, and 84 are the most common COE glasses available for fusing. In general, the lower the COE number, the more time and temperature it will take for the glass to reach the desired state. For example, a glass with a COE of 84 will take more time and a higher temperature to fully fuse than a glass with a COE of 96.

The projects in this book are primarily made from glass with a COE of 96. This glass is easy to cut, available in a wide range of colors and color blends, and fires beautifully in the kiln. A number of glass companies have made 96 COE glass and other fusing components readily available.

Note: If you have other stained glass in your workshop, you will want to set aside a separate area for your fusing glass, leftover scraps, and other fusing supplies. You can always use fusing glass in a regular stained glass project, but you do not want to use regular stained glass in your fusing projects. If you also choose to try fusing glass with other COE numbers, you will need to keep that glass separated from the 96 COE glass.

Just for Fun

Checking glass for compatibility can easily be done with two sheets of polarizing laminated film. Full fuse (1480°F) small squares of the glass you wish to test onto a double layer of clear 96 COE glass.

Place one sheet of the polarizing film on a light source. Lay the test strip across the film and cover with a second sheet of polarizing film. Rotate the top film until the least amount of light is transmitted through the film.

Notice the halos around the glass squares in the top test strip. This indicates that the glass squares were not compatible with the clear 96 COE glass base. In the lower test strip, there are no visible halos around the glass squares. These squares are all 96 COE glass, fully compatible with the clear glass base.

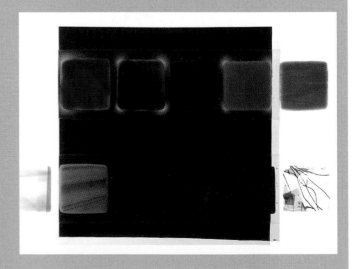

Types of Glass

Clear glass is used in many fusing projects. Thin clear glass is often used in jewelry projects to keep pieces lightweight. Regular 1/8-inch clear glass is useful as a base under a project or a cap over a project. Clear 1/4-inch glass is perfect for a base under projects such as large bowls or platters.

Clear and black glasses also come in interesting textures. You will want to lower your firing temperature when using these kinds of glass to retain as much of the texture as possible.

Transparent colored glass, also called cathedral glass, will brighten any project. You will find a wide variety of shades available, from pastels to vivid hues.

Neutral shades of glass are good background colors and add balance to your work.

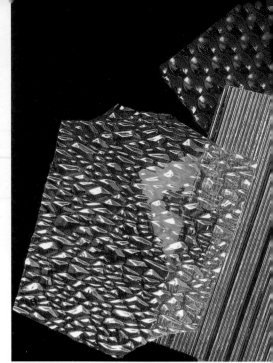

Above: Opal, or opaque glass, can make a bold statement in any project.

Right: Spirit glass comes in fabulous color combinations on both clear and opal bases.

Below: Opal Art glass has wonderful swirls of deep color over a lighter background.

Aventurine glass is available in green, blue, and black. This glass is full of sparkle.

Dichroic glass has a coating that gives the glass a metallic shimmer. Light plays off the reflective coating in a brilliant display of color, making it perfect for jewelry or other small projects. The dichroic surface is available on clear or black background glass, and now is available with interesting patterns and textures.

Iridized glass has a coating on one side that gives the glass a shimmering rainbow effect. To determine which side of the glass has been coated, scratch it with a fingernail. A scratching sound will indicate the iridized side.

Mardi Gras glass combines the look of streamers and frit (tiny grains of glass) on a clear base.

Streaky glass comes in beautiful color combinations that will enhance many projects.

Enhancing Your Projects

There are many products that can be used to accent your projects. Always remember to match the COE number of the accent pieces to the COE of the glass.

Frit. Small pieces of glass that come in various grades or sizes are called frit. In the photo at right, the dark green frit is mosaic size, the red frit is coarse, the dark amber frit is medium, the yellow is fine, and the blue is a powder.

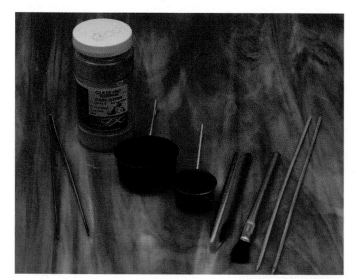

Powdered glass is best applied to a project by using a sifter to drift the fine material onto the glass.

Enamel is even finer than the glass powders. It needs to be mixed with a medium and painted or stamped onto the glass.

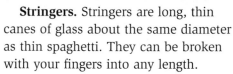

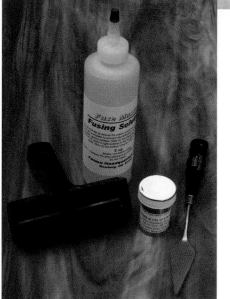

Confetti. This is thin slivers of glass that can be added to the background of a project. Larger pieces can be broken easily with your fingers.

Stringers. Stringers are long, thin canes of glass about the same diameter as thin spaghetti. They can be broken with your fingers into any length.

Noodles. These narrow strips of glass resemble linguine in size and shape. I find it easiest to score them lightly with the glass cutter, and then break them with my fingers.

Bead Rods. These are the glass rods used by bead makers. Because they come in compatible COE numbers, they can also be used as accent pieces in fusing. The best way to cut a bead rod is to use mosaic cutters.

Stringers, noodles, and bead rods are available in a wide range of transparent and opal colors.

FUNDAMENTALS OF GLASS CUTTING

Some fusers began as traditional stained glass crafters and have developed good glass-cutting skills. However, many are new to glass cutting or need a refresher course; this section is for them.

MATERIALS

- [ ] Glass cutter
- [ ] Cutter oil
- [ ] Grozing pliers
- [ ] Running pliers
- [ ] Eight squares of glass, 3 by 3 inches
- [ ] Glass marker
- [ ] Safety glasses

GLASS CUTTERS

There are several styles of glass cutters available, and you will want to invest in one of good quality to ensure your glass-cutting success. Each type of cutter will be held differently.

This upright steel cutter with a ball on top should be held between the first two fingers of your dominant hand.

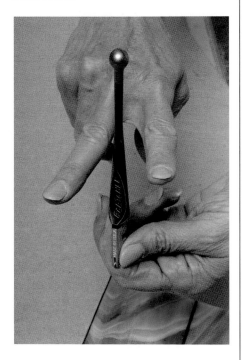

Place your thumb on the indentation at the back of the cutter and your index finger on the front indentation.

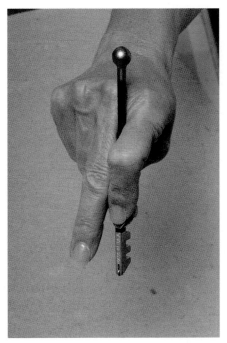

Place the thumb of your opposite hand on the ball at the top of the cutter, while that index finger extends along the cutter head.

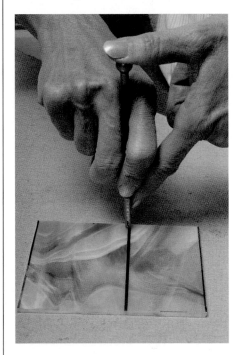

Hold this cutter upright to score the glass. As this cutter has no oil reservoir, you will need to lubricate the cutting wheel. Dip the cutter into a container holding a sponge saturated with cutting oil every few scores.

If you have an upright pencil-shaped cutter designed like this one, hold it in your dominant hand like a pencil.

Place your opposite hand on the other side of the cutter with the index finger extended along the cutter head. This cutter is held at a bit of a slant, much like a pencil. The oil reservoir in this cutter contains cutting oil that lubricates the cutting wheel.

I prefer using a pistol-grip cutter like the one pictured here. It has an oil reservoir to lubricate the cutting wheel, and the design of this cutter helps prevent hand fatigue.

If you are using this oil-fed glass cutter, you will need to put about a teaspoonful of cutting oil in the chamber of the cutter.

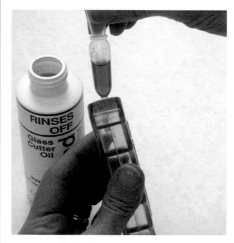

Close the cutter cap gently, as over-tightening can crack the body of the cutter.

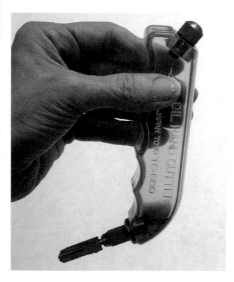

You will hold this glass cutter in your dominant hand and wrap your fingers around it.

Place your other hand around the opposite side of the cutter and extend the index finger of that hand along the cutter head.

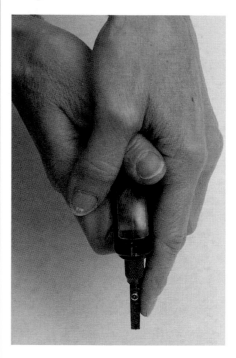

As you progress through the cutting lesson, holding the glass cutter will become more comfortable, so don't worry if this feels awkward.

To begin the cutting practice, you should be standing up. This will put you in a better position to use the proper arm and shoulder muscles needed for scoring glass, and allow you to see over the glass cutter as you work. Wearing safety glasses to protect your vision is always a good idea.

Take a 3-by-3-inch glass square, and draw three lines with the glass marker as indicated in the photo.

Hold the glass cutter so that it is parallel to your work surface. You will be scoring the glass by placing your cutter about ¹/₁₆ inch in from the edge closest to you and moving it across the glass to the opposite edge.

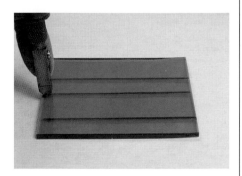

As you look down over the cutter, find the notch that houses the cutting wheel. Center this notch over the black line. Score the glass by moving the glass cutter across the surface of the glass, using a slight downward pressure, and listen for a light scratching sound. Be careful not to use too much pressure. If you notice chips of glass along the score line, you may be pressing too hard.

Stop the score about ¹/₁₆ inch from the far edge of the glass. Stopping here will prevent your cutter from chipping the opposite edge of the glass.

Breaking the Glass

There are three basic ways to break the glass that you have scored. The first method shown is a manual break. Your thumbs should be positioned on either side of the score line, and your fingers will be curled under the glass.

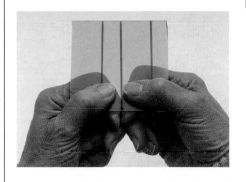

Break the glass as you would break a cracker, pushing upward with your fingers and outward with your thumbs. Always use an outward motion with your thumbs, never a downward motion.

Score the second line drawn on the glass square in the same manner. You will break this score with your grozing pliers. Hold these pliers so that the anvil-shaped edge is on the top and the rounded edge is on the bottom.

Place the grozing pliers perpendicular to the score line, close to but not touching the score. Your other hand will be positioned just opposite the grozing pliers, your thumb near the score line, and your fingers curled under the glass.

Break the glass with the same technique you used in the manual break, pushing upward with your fingers and outward with your thumbs.

Score the remaining line on your glass square. You will break this score with the running pliers. Align the node or line of the running pliers with your score line. This node or line must always be facing upward when using this tool.

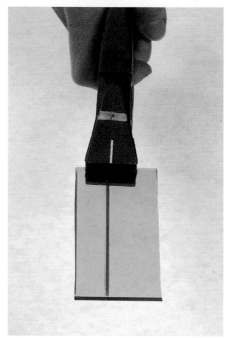

Only about ¼ inch of glass should be held in the jaws of the running pliers.

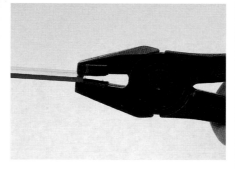

Gently squeeze the handle of the running pliers, and your glass will break apart.

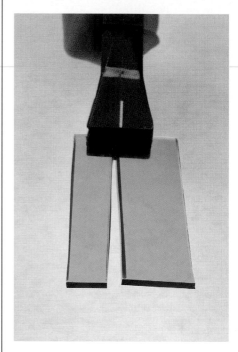

Make sure you try all three methods of breaking a score line. You may become more comfortable with one method over another, but all three breaking techniques are important in working with glass.

Shapes and Curves

Now, let's try cutting some shapes out of glass! The following exercises will help you learn how to cut glass in a variety of shapes for use in fusing projects.

With your glass marker, draw a trapezoid shape similar to shape 1 (see next page) on a 3-by-3-inch squares of glass.

Just as you did when cutting the glass strips, you will need to score the glass, beginning about $1/16$ inch in from the edge of the glass closest to you, and continuing across to the opposite edge. Make sure your cutter head is centered over the black marker line, and remember to stop the score about $1/16$ inch before the opposite edge.

Score only one side of the trapezoid and then break the glass using any one of the three techniques you learned.

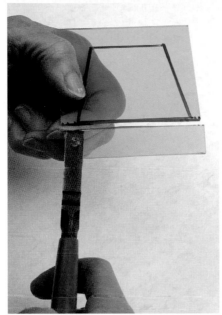

Score the next side of the trapezoid.

Break off that section of glass.

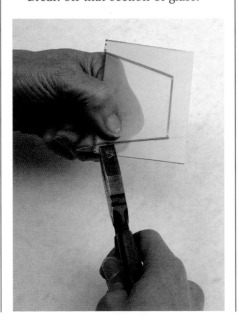

Score and break the third side of the trapezoid.

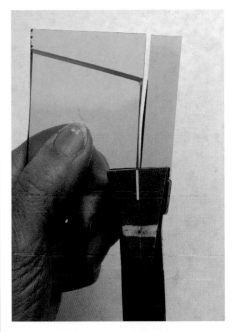

Now, score and break the final side of the trapezoid.

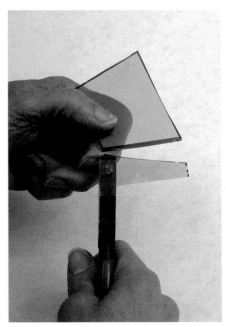

patterns for cutting practice

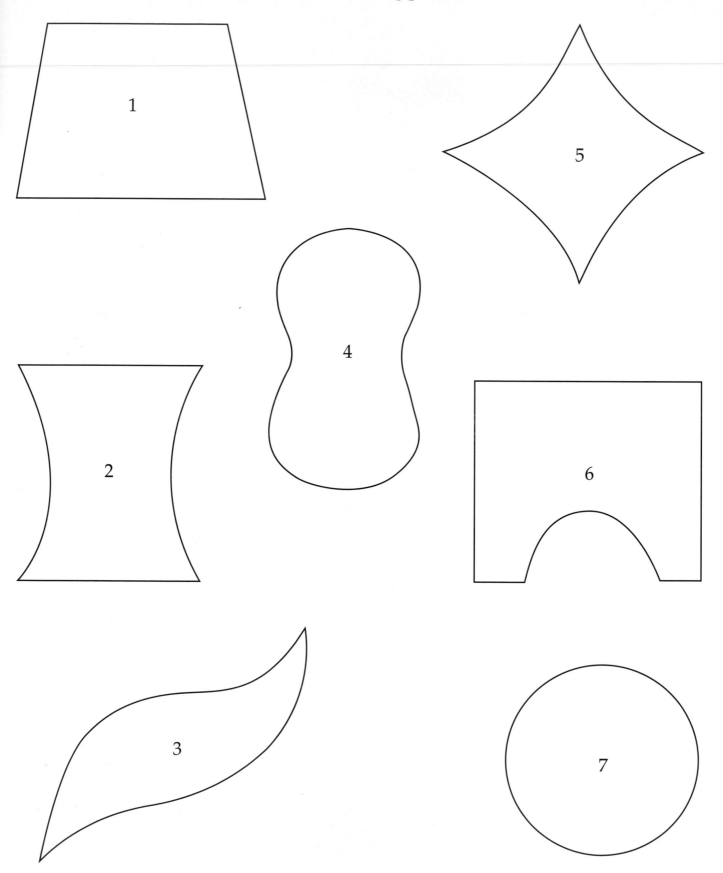

You will now have a completed trapezoid shape. Note that each score was broken before we moved on to the next side. This is an important detail for successful glass cutting.

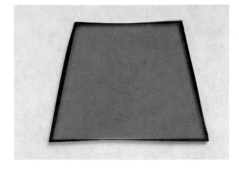

Take another 3-inch square of glass and draw the second shape from the cutting practice designs. You should have two straight sides, and two sides with gentle curves.

Score across one of the straight sides of the drawing, beginning $1/16$ inch in from the edge closest to you, and continuing across the glass to just before the opposite edge.

Break off the glass piece using any method you wish.

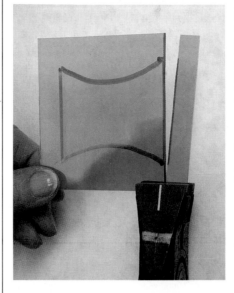

Turn the glass 180 degrees, and make your second score across the other straight side of your drawing. Remember to begin the score just in from the edge closest to you, and stop the score just before the opposite edge.

Break off the excess glass using any method.

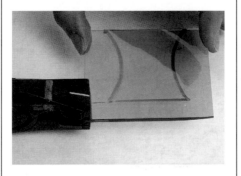

Now, score one of the curved sides of your design.

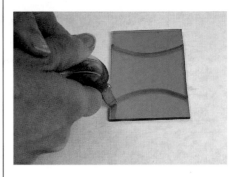

Break off the glass. Note that the grozing pliers are positioned near the base of this score line. You will have better leverage in breaking the glass if you use the grozing pliers at one of the ends of the score line rather than at the midpoint.

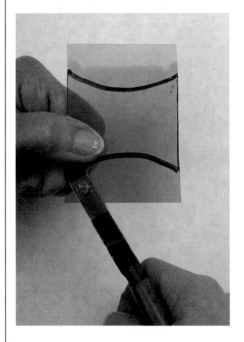

Score the remaining side of your design.

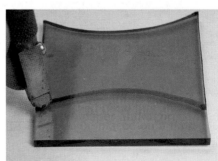

Break off the last piece of glass.

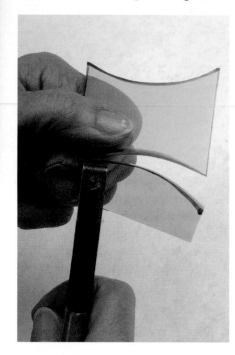

Your finished piece should look something like this.

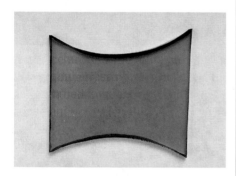

Some of the project designs in this book are floral, so let's try cutting a leaf shape. Draw shape 3 from the cutting practice patterns on one of your glass squares.

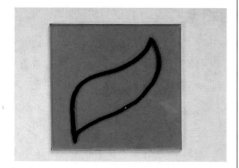

In this shape, the curve of the leaf may be too complex to score and break in one cut. We will score this first side in two sections. Add additional lines with your glass marker similar to the lines shown here.

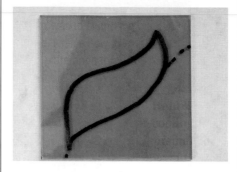

Score along the added line, catching the side of the leaf and then continuing across the second portion of the added line.

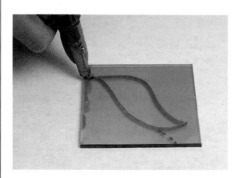

Break off the glass.

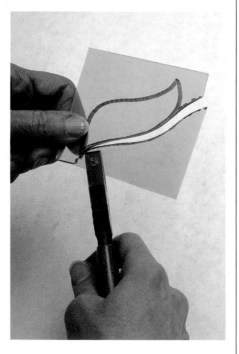

Score across the top of the leaf.

Break off the glass.

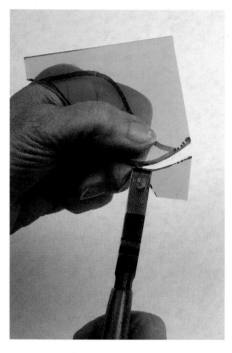

Notice the nub of glass where you started the second score.

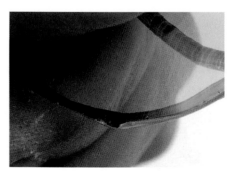

Grasp this nub with your grozing pliers and bend it off for a cleaner look. Try not to crush through the glass.

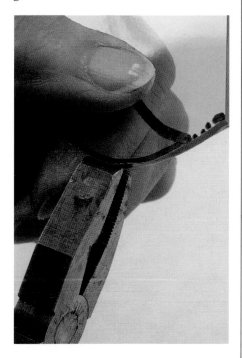

Add another marker line on the opposite side of the leaf, similar to the dotted line shown here.

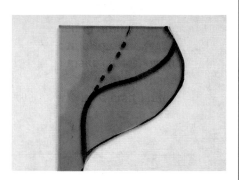

Score the lower portion of the leaf and continue across the glass, following the dotted line.

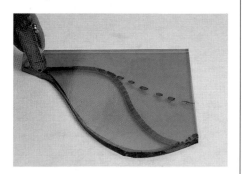

Break off the glass.

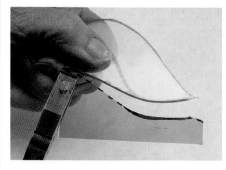

Score the remaining portion of the leaf.

Break off the glass.

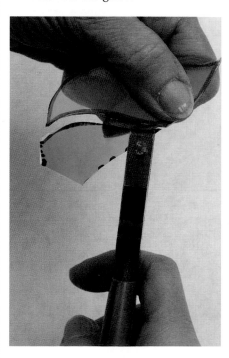

Your finished leaf should look something like this one.

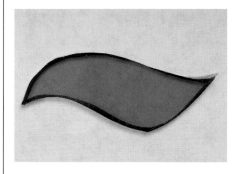

Take another square of glass and draw a peanut-shaped design like shape 4.

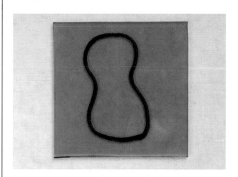

Again, scoring and breaking a piece with this much shape may take additional cuts. Draw a dotted line with your glass marker that begins at the edge of the glass, catches the outer portion of your design, and continues to the opposite edge of the glass.

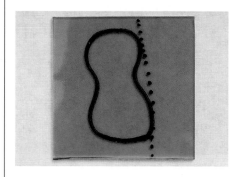

Score the glass, following your added line.

Break away that piece of glass.

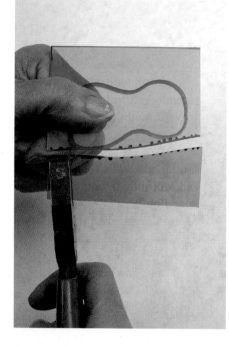

Now you can score the inner curve of that side.

Break off the excess glass.

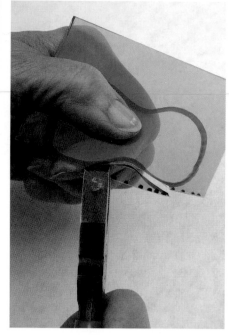

Draw a similar dotted line on the left side of your design. Again, you will begin at the edge of the glass, catch the rounded sides of the design, and continue to the opposite edge of the glass.

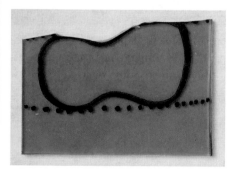

Score along the dotted line.

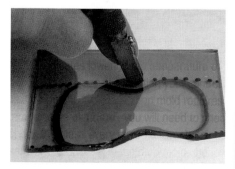

Break the glass.

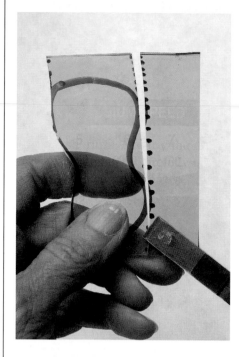

Score the inner curve.

Break the glass.

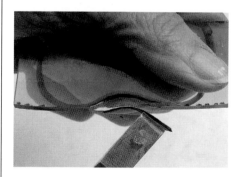

Score and break off one of the outer curved ends of your design.

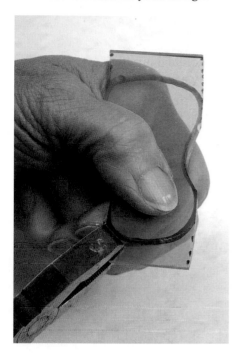

Repeat the score and break on the final side of your design.

Your finished shape should be similar to the one shown here.

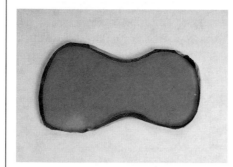

Shape 5 is a four-pointed star. Draw this shape on another of your glass squares.

Use your glass marker to add a dotted line that begins at the edge of the glass closest to you, catches the inner curve of your design, and continues to the right edge of the glass.

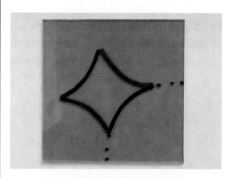

Score the glass along this line.

Break off the excess glass. Notice that the grozing pliers are still positioned at the beginning of the score line.

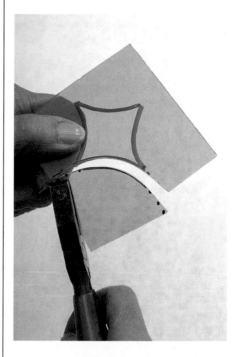

Draw another dotted line that catches the next curve of your design and continues to the edge of the glass.

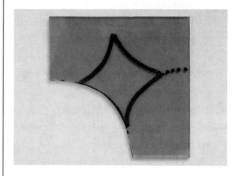

Score and break the glass on this second curve.

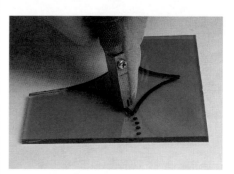

Go on to the third side of the star, scoring and breaking the glass in a similar fashion.

Finally, score and break the fourth side of the star.

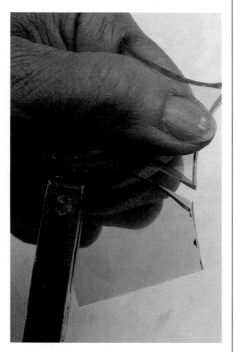

Your finished star should look similar to this one.

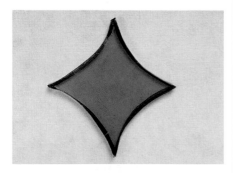

Let's move on to shape 6. Draw this design on one of the glass squares. With a shape like this one, it becomes very important to cut the

section of the design with the deep inside curve first. The glass along the straight sides of the design will add extra support while we are working on this curve. This will be a rule to remember throughout your entire glass-cutting career.

Draw a dotted line across the glass, catching the lower lines of the design.

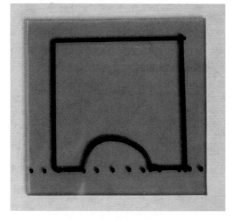

Score the glass along this line.

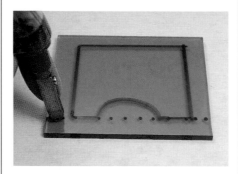

Break the scored glass.

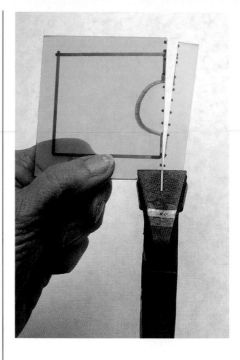

In the inner curve, draw a smaller arch.

Score along the smaller arch.

Break out this small piece of glass. Your grozing pliers are the best tool for this break.

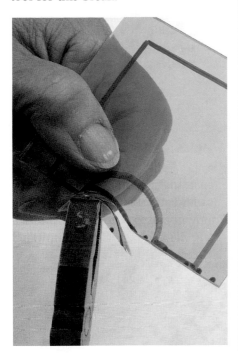

From the opposite side of the inner curve, draw another smaller arch.

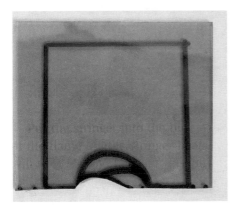

Score along the smaller arch.

Break out the small piece of glass.

Now score along the top of the original inner curve.

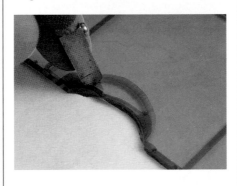

Break the final piece of glass from the arch.

With the more difficult part of the design cut, you can easily score and break the straight sides of your design.

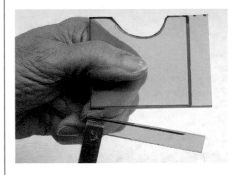

Your finished shape should look like this.

The final practice shape to cut will be a circle. Draw or trace a circle on your glass square.

Use the glass marker to draw a dotted line that starts at the edge of the glass closest to you, goes around a portion of the circle, and continues to the edge of the glass.

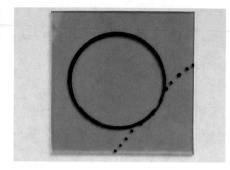

Score the glass, following your drawn line.

Break off this section of glass.

Draw another line that catches the next arc of the circle, and continues to the side of the glass. Score along this line.

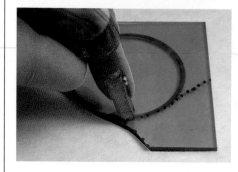

Break off the glass piece.

Continue this technique around the remaining portion of the circle. It should take five or six scores and breaks to cut out the entire circle.

Your finished circle will look similar to this one. Notice that you have some rough edges where each break was. We will address those rough spots in the next section when we discuss grinding the glass. You can also practice the technique where you grasp the nub of glass with your grozing pliers and bend it off.

Let's look at your practice pieces. Are you getting more comfortable with cutting and breaking the glass?

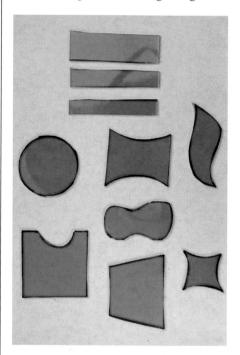

As you are cutting shapes of glass for your projects, you may find that some of the edges aren't quite smooth. You may need to grind the edges of the glass to perfect their shapes. A glass grinder is a good addition to your workshop.

We will use our circle from the glass cutting practice section as an example. Notice the burrs of glass on the edges of the circle.

Refer to your grinder's instruction manual to set up the grinder and fill the reservoir with water. Make sure that the cooling sponge is wet and in contact with the water reservoir as well as the grinder head. Always keep the eye shield in place when using the grinder and wear safety glasses to protect your eyes. Read the additional safety notes in the instruction manual.

Turn on the grinder. While keeping the glass flat on the grinder deck, gently press the glass piece against the rotating grinder head.

Always move the glass in a left to right motion (though with a circle like this, it will be a clockwise direction), using just enough pressure to keep the glass in contact with the grinder head. Avoid scrubbing the glass against the grinder head, as this scrubbing motion may cause the glass to chip. Continue to grind around the entire circle.

Pro Tip: More exact cutting comes with practice. The more proficient you become with your cutting skills, the less grinding you will need to do!

After grinding, the circle has much smoother edges.

In some cases, you may need to grind a piece of glass with a pattern glued in place. Grind the glass just to the edge of the pattern paper, but not beyond.

Special Cutting Techniques

Cutting Squares or Rectangles

Many fused glass projects begin with a square or rectangular base. You can easily measure and cut one from a sheet of glass using a ruler and a square. First, make sure that your left edge and the bottom edge of the glass are straight. If not, trim those edges to give yourself a good starting point.

Measure the width of glass you need for your project. Here, we will be cutting an 8 1/2-inch square from light blue glass for our Embossed Plate. Measure and mark a point 8 1/2 inches in from the left edge of the glass.

For accuracy, measure and mark two additional points the same distance in from the left edge.

Place the ridge of the square against the lower edge of the glass, with the side of the square close to your three markings. You will need to allow about a 1/16-inch space between the marks and the straight edge of the square to compensate for the glass cutter head.

Score along the square's straight edge.

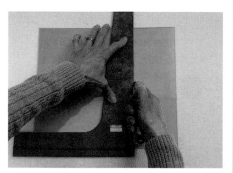

Break the glass.

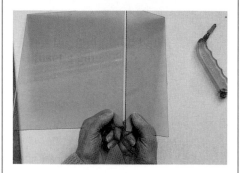

Turn the glass on its side and make a mark 8 1/2 inches from the new left edge. Again, mark two additional points for accuracy.

Line up the edge of the square with your three marks. Once again, you will need to leave 1/16 inch between your marks and the straight edge to compensate for the glass cutter head.

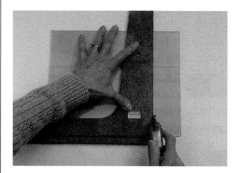

Score and break the glass.

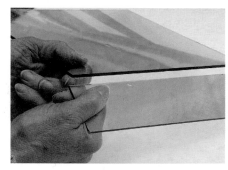

You should have a perfect 8 1/2-inch square for your project.

2

Using a Kiln

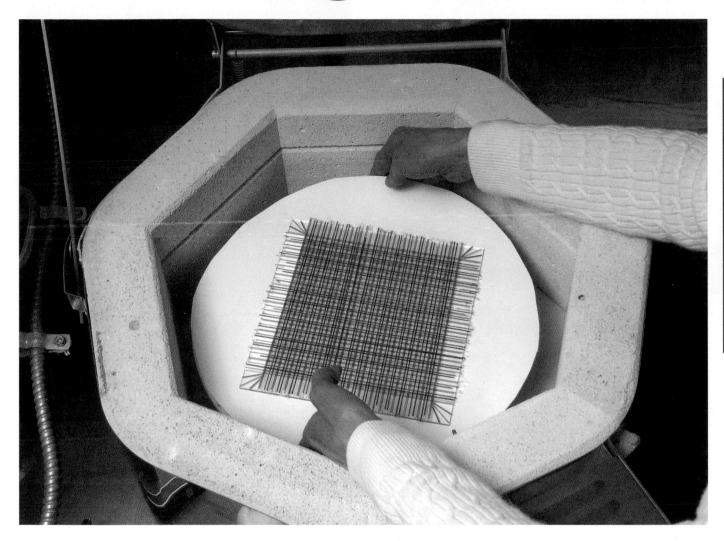

Choosing a kiln that is right for you can be a challenging decision, as this will be your greatest investment. There are numerous quality manufacturers offering a wide variety of kilns. A visit to your local glass retailer to discuss kilns can be very helpful in determining the features that will be most useful to you.

One of your first considerations when selecting a kiln should be size. You will want a kiln large enough to accommodate your projects, but not so large that you are heating extra space during most of your firings. Small tabletop kilns are great for firing pieces like jewelry or small tiles. These kilns will generally use a shelf that can be from 5 inches square up to 8 inches square. If you plan to make bowls and plates, you will want to look for a kiln with a midsize chamber and a shelf that is 12 to 14 inches in diameter. Larger platters, sinks, or deep drop pieces will require a larger kiln. The depth of the chamber will also be important if you plan to work with projects of this size.

Using a Kiln

KILN CONTROLLERS

There are two basic types of controllers for kilns: manual and automatic. Manual controllers must be operated by turning a dial to the desired level, and continuing to increase that level during the firing process. This isn't a difficult task, but it requires you to remain with the kiln throughout the entire firing and annealing stages. (See page 10 for an explanation of the annealing process.)

An automatic controller can be programmed to heat and cool the kiln according to your firing schedule. This gives you a bit more freedom to work on other projects while firing the kiln. Some kilns with automatic controllers come with factory-installed programs plus the capacity to add and store programs of your own.

This automatic controller on my small kiln, at right, is easy to program and adjust to fine-tune a firing process.

My midsize kiln controller, shown below, has a different layout but is also very easy to program.

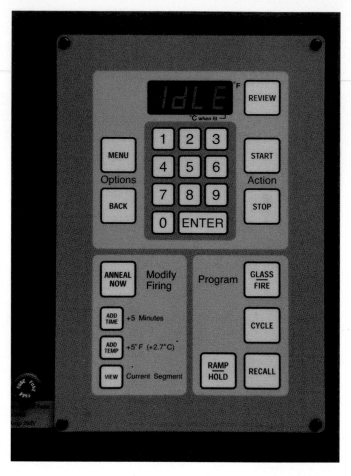

ELECTRICAL CONSIDERATIONS

Electrical service is an important factor when choosing a kiln. Small to midsize kilns often use 120-volt service while larger kilns may require 240-volt service. Make sure you will be able to accommodate the service that your kiln requires. If in doubt, consult an electrician for advice.

Your kiln should be set up close to an electrical outlet so that the cord can be plugged directly into the socket. Extension cords are not recommended for use with kilns.

HEATING ELEMENTS

Another feature to consider when choosing a kiln is the location of the heating elements within the kiln.

The small kiln at right has the heating coils on the side walls. Baffles are inserted to prevent accidental contact with the coils.

In the kiln below, the heating elements are located in the lid. Many fusers prefer the heat source above the glass so they can obtain a glossy finish on their projects.

My largest kiln has heating elements in both the lid and around the sides of the chamber. This provides for a very even heat distribution throughout the chamber of the kiln.

KILN SHELF

All projects need to be fired on a kiln shelf for support. Many shelves are made from mullite or clay materials, which provide a very smooth surface for firing. Another option for a kiln shelf would be fiber board, an alumina silica product. Shelves made from fiber board are generally lightweight, but the surface may not be as smooth as a shelf made from mullite or clay.

KILN OPENINGS

The opening of a kiln makes a difference in how a project is loaded onto the shelf. With a front-load kiln, a small project can easily be slid into the chamber.

Placing a project in a top-load kiln is also simple. The advantage here is that you can visually check your work to make sure the glass and components have not shifted during their transfer from your work table to the kiln.

A third option is the clamshell kiln. On this type of kiln, the lid opens from the bottom to expose the shelf. This provides easy access to the shelf area for setting up a project.

KILN WASH

Kiln wash is a shelf primer used to prevent glass from sticking to the kiln shelf or slumping mold. It generally comes as a powder that you mix with water then apply to the mold or shelf with a soft brush such as a Haik brush.

Metal molds require special attention. This spray mold release works well and you will learn how to use it in the project section.

KILN POSTS

Also made from ceramic material or mullite clay, kiln posts are placed between the kiln shelf and the floor of the kiln's firing chamber. Raising the kiln shelf in this manner allows air to circulate under the kiln shelf for even heat distribution. Place three kiln posts in a triangular configuration for the most stable shelf support.

FIBER PAPER

Fiber paper can be used in place of kiln paper if you want to add texture to the back of your glass. It also will be used in the embossing projects later in this book. The top fiber paper in the photo at left is $1/8$ inch thick, and the bottom fiber paper is $1/16$ inch thick.

KILN PAPER

This material acts as a separator between the glass and the kiln shelf. It contains ceramic fibers to prevent the glass from sticking to the kiln shelf and is used in addition to kiln wash. A piece of thin kiln paper over your prepared kiln shelf also helps prevent air bubbles from forming under the glass and prolongs the life of the kiln wash on your shelf.

SLUMPING AND DRAPING MOLDS

Generally, glass is *slumped* into a ceramic mold, as the glass contracts a bit more than the ceramic material. With care, a ceramic mold will endure hundreds of firings.

Glass is most often *draped* over the outside of a stainless steel mold, as the metal contracts a bit more than the glass. These molds can last for years and years.

At times, you may wish to make your own mold to create a particular shape. The fiber board above was easily carved into the drop mold used in the floral drop vase project, and it can also be used to carve casting molds. Glass can be fired over or into a fiber board mold. Fluffy fiber blanket can be formed into shape, and when dampened with fiber mold hardener, it will become a rigid mold.

KILN SHELF PREPARATION

Your kiln shelf needs to have a smooth surface. Any chips in the kiln wash will show up as uneven areas on the back of your fired project. Notice the areas shown where the kiln wash has flaked away. This shelf needs to be completely cleaned, and to have new kiln wash applied.

To do this first, scrape the old kiln wash from the shelf with a mesh screen. You can brush it straight into a trash bin.

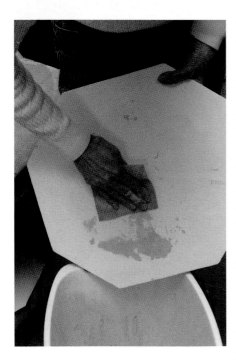

Note: It is very important to wear a dust mask when cleaning a shelf or handling kiln wash.

Now, scrub any remaining kiln wash from the shelf with warm water. You need to scrub the shelf down to the bare surface.

Dry the shelf with a towel and allow it to air-dry overnight.

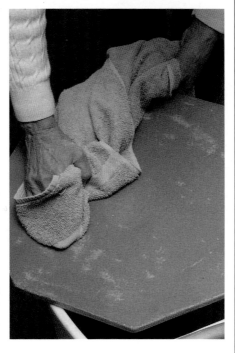

When the shelf is completely dry, it is time to apply fresh kiln wash. Generally, I mix 1 part of the kiln wash with 4 to 5 parts of water, but check the manufacturer's directions for your specific type of kiln wash. Mix well. You will notice this particular brand of kiln wash is pink. Once the shelf has been prefired, the kiln wash will appear white.

Apply the kiln wash with a soft brush such as this Haik brush. Our first layer is applied vertically.

After the first layer has soaked into the shelf, apply the second layer of kiln wash perpendicular to the first one.

Allow the liquid to soak into the shelf, and then apply a diagonal layer of kiln wash in each direction.

Finish with another vertical and another horizontal application for a total of six layers of kiln wash solution.

Allow the kiln wash to air-dry. You will then need to prefire the shelf to 500°F and hold it at that temperature for twelve minutes. When the kiln has cooled to 100°F or less, the prepared shelf can be removed from the kiln and used to fire your project. Notice that the kiln wash has turned white during the firing.

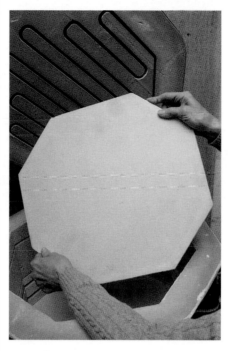

Notes: The kiln shelf must be level for your glass project to fire evenly. To check this, place a level on the shelf and adjust your kiln setup accordingly.

MOLD PREPARATION

Preparing a slumping mold is very similar to preparing the kiln shelf. The first layer of kiln wash is applied in one direction.

Apply the next layer perpendicular to the first.

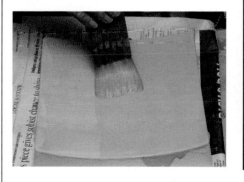

Apply a diagonal layer in each direction.

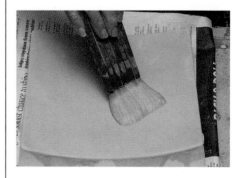

End with additional vertical and horizontal layers of kiln wash for a total of six layers. Remember to brush some kiln wash around the sides of the mold as well.

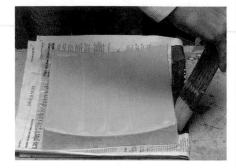

Open any vent holes in the mold with a toothpick.

I have placed my mold on a shelf to air-dry. The pink color is a good reminder that this mold will need to be prefired to 500°F before it can be used to slump glass.

FUSING ADHESIVES

I avoid using fusing adhesives whenever possible, but sometimes it becomes necessary to use a product to keep glass from shifting during the transfer of a project from the work table to the kiln shelf. You can use fuser's glue, white glue thinned with water, or hairspray from a pump container to keep the components in place. Avoid aerosol sprays as they contain additional propellants that may not fire cleanly away.

Proper use of fusing glue and hairspray is shown in the project section of this book. Look for this information in the orchid tile garden stake project (page 39).

CLEANING THE GLASS

It is important to clean all glass pieces before firing a project. Oil from your glass cutter, debris from the grinder, and fingerprints will need to be removed.

Glass should be washed in warm water mixed with a mild detergent, rinsed well, and dried. Some fusers find that rubbing alcohol and lint-free paper towels are also useful cleaning supplies.

Fired projects should be cleaned carefully. Once the projects have cooled, dip them into a basin of water, allowing any kiln wash residue or kiln paper to sink to the bottom of the basin. The clear water can be poured off slowly, and the sediment can be scraped into a trash bin.

There are a few general safety practices that will keep glass fusing an enjoyable experience.

- First, be careful when handling the glass. The edges can be sharp and will become even sharper as you cut the glass. Use a bench brush to keep your work surface clean, and brush away any scraps or debris.

- Wear safety glasses when cutting or grinding glass pieces to protect your vision.

- Kiln gloves and arm protection are necessities. Wear them when opening a hot kiln.

- Wear a dust mask when working with kiln wash or glass powders, or when disposing of fired kiln paper.

- Kiln paper contains ceramic fibers and needs to be handled with care. Once kiln paper has been fired, it turns into a cottonlike substance that cannot be lifted from the shelf. To dispose of used kiln paper, slide it off the shelf into a trash bin.

- Set up your kiln on a solid, nonflammable surface at least 18 inches from all surrounding walls. Keep the kiln area free from paper and debris.

Let's start with some basic fusing terminology to familiarize you with the firing processes.

Fusing. Using time and temperature to heat glass pieces until they bond together. The following temperature ranges apply to glass with a Coefficient of Expansion of 96, the type of glass I use in my studio. If you choose to work with glass with a different COE, the temperatures for each process may vary. Test fire a sample of glass prior to firing an intricate project to ensure the firing temperatures will give you the look you want.

There are three basic levels of fusing:
- *Tack fuse.* Heating the glass pieces to the point where they will stick together but not enough to change their original shapes (1350°F–1400°F).
- *Contour Fuse.* Heating the glass pieces to a temperature where they bond together and the edges become soft and rounded (1400°F–1440°F).
- *Full Fuse.* Heating the glass to a temperature where all the pieces are fully melted together. The top surface of the glass will be smooth and glossy, and the edges will have a completely rounded look (1450°F–1480°F).

Sagging. Heating the glass to a temperature warm enough to change its shape. There are two kinds of sagging:
- *Slumping.* Sagging the glass into a mold until it takes the shape of that mold (1225 °F–1250°F).
- *Draping.* Sagging the glass over the outside of a mold (1225°F–1250°F).

Annealing. The slow cooling of glass through a temperature range to ensure a stable finished product that is free from stress.

Glass contracts as it cools. If the top surface of the glass cools more quickly than the interior of the glass, stress builds and may cause the glass to break. If the cooling process is controlled by holding the temperature at a certain level for a period of time, all the glass molecules can reach the same temperature, eliminating the stress. For 96 COE glass, the annealing range is between 960°F and 975°F.

Pro Tip: Avoid opening the kiln when the temperature reading is between 950°F and 1100°F. This is the critical strain zone in the heating process and the annealing zone during the cooling process. Exposing the project to room-temperature air could cause a thermal shock, resulting in a cracked or broken project.

Hold Time/Soak Time. A period during the heating or cooling cycle during which the temperature of the kiln is held at a particular level. This allows all molecules of the glass to reach the same temperature and prevents stress from building in the glass.

I've made four similar tiles to show the difference firing temperatures can make in your finished projects.

This first tile was fired to a tack fuse temperature of 1375°F. You can see how the edges of the glass have barely softened, and the glass base fully retains its shape.

Pro Tip: Although most fusing glass is ⅛ inch thick, its more natural state is ¼ inch. Given enough time and temperature in the kiln, glass will pull in at the edges working toward that depth. This works to your advantage when you are making nuggets and jewelry pieces that you want well rounded, but it may not give you the desired results on a tile. Reduce your top firing temperature or add a second layer of base glass to prevent distortion at the glass edges.

Using a Kiln

The next tile was fired to a contour fuse temperature of 1420°F. The edges of the glass have a softer look at this temperature, and the base glass has begun to change shape a bit.

This tile has been fired to a full fuse temperature of 1480°F. The design pieces have completely melted into the base glass. Notice how the outer edges of the base have pulled in around the design.

Note: Every kiln's firing process is a little bit different, so you will need to experiment with your kiln to find what temperature produces the results you like. Keep written records of your projects, noting the firing temperatures used for your future reference.

The final tile was fired to a full fuse temperature of 1480°F as well, but this time, I added a second layer of base glass. This helps to minimize the distortion at the edges of the base glass. Again, the design pieces have completely melted into the base glass.

At these various firing temperatures, the tiles fired to the look I expected.

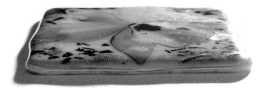

Using a Kiln

FIRING SCHEDULES

A firing schedule involves three components: the *rate* (number of degrees per hour) at which you want the temperature to increase or decrease, the *temperature* (in degrees Fahrenheit) you wish to reach at each stage, and the *hold time* (in minutes) at which you want to maintain that top temperature.

Some fusers set the rate of their firing and heat straight up to the top temperature of their program. I tend to use a more conservative firing schedule, which allows for hold times during the heating process as well as the cooling stages. The firing process may take a little longer, but the results are consistently positive. You have spent time designing and making your project; be patient throughout the firing process, and your finished project will reflect the time you invested.

The projects in this book include firing directions. If your kiln has factory-set programs, you will be able to use them. A reference back to these firing schedules is also included if you want to set up your own custom programs.

Pro Tip: Always check your work as it nears the top temperature of your firing program. It is simple to adjust the top temperature or hold time during a firing; check your kiln manual for directions. With a quick peek into the kiln, you can prevent overfiring a project, or having to refire it to achieve your desired results.

FIRING SCHEDULE A—TACK FUSE, MEDIUM SPEED

	1	2	3	4	5	6	7	8
Rate (degrees/hour)	500	500	500	600	600	9999*	100	100
Top Temperature (°F)	300	600	960	1240	1375	1000	960	750
Hold Time (minutes)	12	12	20	30	12	30	45	01

FIRING SCHEDULE B—CONTOUR FUSE, MEDIUM SPEED

	1	2	3	4	5	6	7	8
Rate (degrees/hour)	500	500	500	600	600	9999*	100	100
Top Tempterature (°F)	300	600	960	1240	1400–1420	1000	960	750
Hold Time (minutes)	12	12	20	30	12	45	60	01

FIRING SCHEDULE C—FULL FUSE, MEDIUM SPEED

	1	2	3	4	5	6	7	8
Rate (degrees/hour)	500	500	500	600	600	9999*	100	100
Top Temperature (°F)	300	600	960	1240	1480	1000	960	750
Hold Time (minutes)	12	12	20	30	12	30	45	01

FIRING SCHEDULE D—FULL FUSE, SLOW SPEED

	1	2	3	4	5	6	7	8
Rate (degrees/hour)	300	300	300	600	600	9999*	100	100
Top Temperature (°F)	300	600	960	1240	1480	1000	960	750
Hold Time (minutes)	15	15	30	45	12	45	60	01

FIRING SCHEDULE E—SLUMP, SLOW SPEED

	1	2	3	4	5	6	7
Rate (degrees/hour)	300	300	300	600	9999*	100	100
Top Temperature (°F)	300	600	960	1250	1000	960	750
Hold Time (minutes)	20	20	30	12	45	60	01

FIRING SCHEDULE F—DROP MOLD SLUMP, SLOW SPEED

	1	2	3	4	5	6	7
Rate (degrees/hour)	300	300	300	500	9999*	100	100
Top Temperature (°F)	300	600	960	1250	1000	960	750
Hold Time (minutes)	20	20	30	60-180**	60	60	01

*9999 indicates lowering the temperature of the kiln as quickly as possible. Check your kiln manual for the specific notation your controller will show.

** Slumping glass over a drop mold requires close attention. When the glass reaches the top temperature of 1250°F, you will need to check the drop's progress often. Set a timer and check the glass every fifteen to twenty minutes until the glass reaches the kiln shelf. The smaller the opening in the drop mold, the longer it seems to take for the glass to drop.

Nuggets

Commercially made 96 COE glass nuggets are a wonderful addition to many projects, but sometimes you may want a size or color that isn't available. Making your own nuggets is an easy alternative. The nuggets we are preparing to make will be used in our Vintage Wine Cellar Sign.

Cut strips of 96 COE glass approximately ¼ inch wide. Use mosaic cutters to nip off ¼-inch segments from the glass strips.

Cut a large number of these segments so you will be able to fill the kiln shelf. There is no need to grind the edges of these glass pieces, as the heat of the kiln will round the glass into perfect circles.

Place a sheet of thin kiln paper on your prepared kiln shelf. Stack two pieces of the glass for each nugget. Keep the stacks about ½ inch apart to keep them from melting into one another.

Prepare your kiln for firing. Use firing schedule C from page 34 or the following firing guidelines.

Firing Guidelines

Speed: Medium
Process: Full Fuse
Top Temp: 1480°F
Hold Time: 20 Minutes

I checked these nuggets at their top temperature of 1480°F. At this high temperature, the glass and the kiln heating elements are glowing red-hot.

After firing, allow the kiln temperature to cool to 100°F or less before opening the lid. You should find that your glass nuggets are perfectly rounded and ready to use in your favorite projects.

Be sure to wash any kiln paper residue from the back of the glass nuggets. Allow the residue to settle to the bottom of your rinse basin, pour off the clear water, and dispose of the sediment by scraping it into the trash bin.

Bending Stringers and Noodles

Some of the projects presented in this book use bent stringers or noodles as design accents. They will add some pizzazz to your work and are not difficult to make if you use a good heat source such as a bead torch.

Remove the plastic cap from the MAPP gas and screw the torch head onto the tank.

Slip the hose clamp around the tank and slide the L bracket into position.

Tighten the hose clamp with the screwdriver until it is secure.

Use the quick-release clamp to firmly attach the L bracket to the edge of your work table.

MATERIALS

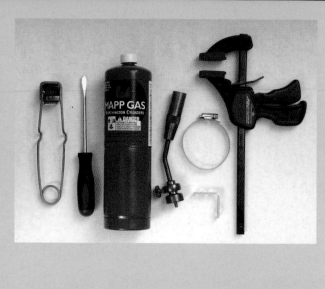

- [ ] Hot Head torch head
- [ ] MAPP gas tank
- [ ] Hose clamp
- [ ] L bracket
- [ ] Quick-release clamp
- [ ] Striker
- [ ] Screwdriver
- [ ] Two pairs of tweezers
- [ ] Assorted stringers and noodles

Note: If you are not familiar with setting up and using a bead torch, please seek advice from an experienced bead maker or your local stained glass shop that carries bead-making supplies.

The bead torch can seem intimidating. If using this technique does not appeal to you, you can get a similar effect using a candle flame. Because the candle flame is much cooler than the torch flame, you will need to be patient—do not bend the stringer before the glass is warm enough to manipulate or it will break.

Hold the striker in your dominant hand and use your other hand to turn the valve that opens the gas tank.

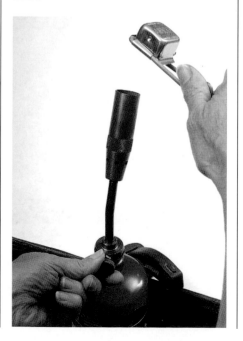

As soon as you hear the hiss of the gas escaping, use the striker to light the flame.

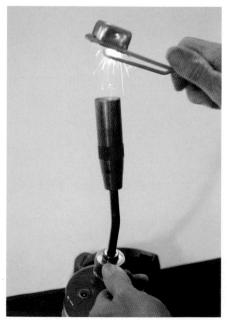

Adjust the gas flow until the blue flame is about 1½ inches long.

Pick up one end of a stringer in your left hand and hold the other end with a pair of tweezers in your right hand.

Put the stringer into the blue part of the flame. As the stringer heats, it will turn red and become very pliable.

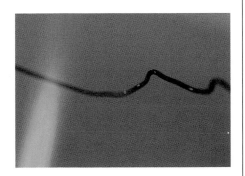

Move your right hand to create bends and twists in the stringer.

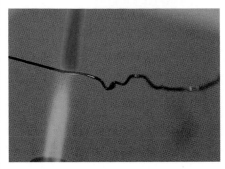

If the stringer becomes too soft, bring it forward out of the flame for a few seconds to allow the glass to cool.

Continue bending the entire length of stringer. When your left hand gets too close to the flame, use the second pair of tweezers to hold that end of the stringer.

This same technique can be used to bend glass noodles. The process will take a little longer than bending stringers as you will have more glass to heat.

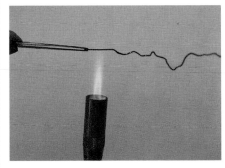

Pro Tip: You can make short segments of bent stringers by holding the stringer in the flame and gently pulling it apart. The flame will cut the stringer.

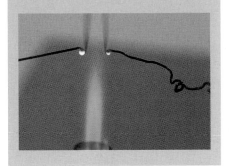

Cutting a noodle in the torch flame is also very similar to cutting a stringer. Again, hold the noodle in the flame until the glass is molten. Then pull the ends of the glass apart.

Bend more stringers and noodles than you need for your current project. You will be reaching for extra pieces to enhance lots of future projects!

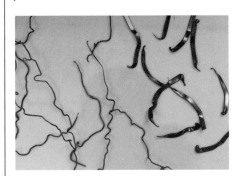

3
Projects

This garden stake will look great in a large potted plant or in any outdoor garden setting.

The pattern can be found on page 141.

- Making a Tile
- Using Frit, Glass Powder, and Confetti
- Using Adhesives

Projects

39

- ☐ Glass for base: a 4¼-inch square
- ☐ Glass for orchid: ⅓ square foot
- ☐ Pattern
- ☐ Fuser's glue or white glue thinned with water
- ☐ Toothpick
- ☐ Light amber powder
- ☐ Yellow opal fine frit
- ☐ Black opal medium frit
- ☐ Forest green confetti
- ☐ Tweezers
- ☐ Clean brush
- ☐ Small scoop
- ☐ Powder sifter
- ☐ Scissors
- ☐ Rubber cement or glass marker
- ☐ Glass-cutting tools
- ☐ Thin kiln paper
- ☐ Prepared kiln shelf

1. Make a copy of the pattern pieces for this project and cut them out with scissors. You can either glue these pattern pieces onto the glass with rubber cement, or use them as a template and draw around them on the glass with a glass marker.

Cut out the glass pieces and grind the edges. Wash, rinse, and dry the pieces of glass of the design as well as the base glass for the project. Arrange the orchid pieces on the base glass.

2. Pour a small amount of fuser's glue or thinned white glue on a scrap of glass.

Dip the end of the toothpick into the fuser's glue.

Pick up one of your design pieces, then touch the toothpick to it. This trace amount of glue is all you need.

Replace the glass piece onto the base.

3. Continue gluing the remaining design pieces onto the base.

4. Once the design pieces have all been glued into position, you are ready to decorate your tile. Use a small scoop to pick up some fine yellow opal frit.

Drop the frit in the center of the orchid.

You can use a clean, dry brush to push the frit together.

Pro Tip: Use fusing glue or any adhesive sparingly. Too much glue can cause carbon deposits between the glass layers. These will become black splotches that can never be removed after kiln firing.

5. Scoop some light amber powder and place it in a small powder sifter.

Rub a pencil or other tool over the twisted handle of the sifter so that a fine drifting of powder falls onto your base glass.

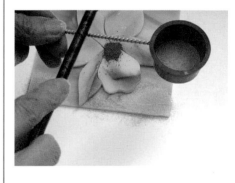

Projects

41

Try to get a very light dusting of powder around your design.

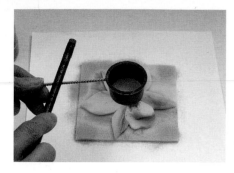

6. Break the confetti into small pieces with your fingers. Sprinkle the confetti around the flower petals.

7. Add a few pieces of black frit to the yellow frit in the orchid's center. Using a pair of tweezers can make placement of small accents a bit easier.

8. Place the tile on a prepared kiln shelf covered with a piece of thin kiln paper. Your tile is now ready to fire.

9. Use firing schedule A from page 34 or the following firing guidelines.

Firing Guidelines

Speed: Medium
Process: Tack Fuse
Top Temp: 1375°F
Hold Time: 12 Minutes

10. After you have fired the glass tile, you must allow the kiln to cool to 100°F or less before opening the kiln and removing your project. Carefully wash any residue from kiln paper in your rinse basin. Allow the particles to settle to the bottom of the container, pour off the clear water, and dispose of the sediment in a trash bin.

We have chosen to display the orchid tile in a mini garden stake. Here's how you attach the tile to the metal stake.

Place a small dot of the adhesive in each corner of the inner rim of the garden stake.

Set the orchid tile in position and gently press the glass into the adhesive.

Place the garden tile on a flat surface and allow the adhesive to set for at least 24 hours. Your orchid garden stake will be a perfect addition to your flower garden.

MATERIALS

- [ ] Finished tile
- [ ] E6000 adhesive or other silicone adhesive
- [ ] Mini garden stake with a 4¼-inch opening

This snowman design makes a great tile that you can use in several ways. If you wish to just hang the tile after fusing, you may want to add a hook before firing the glass. I've made my tile into a candleholder to chase away the winter chill.

The pattern can be found on page 142.

- Using Glass Stringers and Noodles
- Combining Fused Glass with Traditional Stained Glass

MATERIALS

- [ ] 4 x 5-inch clear iridized granite glass
- [ ] White opal glass: scrap
- [ ] Aventurine blue glass: scrap
- [ ] Sunflower yellow glass: scrap
- [ ] White opal medium frit
- [ ] Iridized clear medium frit
- [ ] Sky blue fine frit
- [ ] Aventurine black medium frit
- [ ] Black coarse frit
- [ ] Light amber stringer
- [ ] Black noodle
- [ ] Black stringer
- [ ] Bent stringers—any colors
- [ ] Yellow opal noodle
- [ ] Glass-cutting tools
- [ ] Pattern
- [ ] Glass marker
- [ ] Hairspray (pump container)
- [ ] Thin kiln paper
- [ ] Prepared kiln shelf

Projects

1. Using the pattern as a template, trace the snowman's body and head on the white glass.

2. Score and break the glass.

3. Grind the snowman's body and head to smooth the edges.

4. Trace the hat and hatband designs onto the aventurine blue glass. Cut and grind these pieces.

5. Trace the snowman's nose onto the scrap of sunflower yellow glass. Cut this small piece and grind it if there are any rough edges.

6. Wash, rinse, and dry all glass pieces, including the base glass.

7. Assemble the snowman on the smooth side of the 4 x 5-inch iridized clear base.

8. Measure and mark a yellow noodle to use for a hat band.

Gently score the noodle with your glass cutter and break it at the score with your fingers.

Position the noodle over the seam between the hat top and the hat bottom.

9. Break pieces of a black stringer for the snowman's arms and cut a piece of black noodle for the broomstick.

Pro Tip: Tweezers are especially helpful when trying to position small pieces. Use them to place stringers, frit, noodles, and small pieces of glass.

10. Give your snowman hands with small segments of a black stringer.

11. Use a bent stringer for the scarf (see Chapter 2, Preparing Accent Components, for directions on how to bend a stringer).

12. Use small segments of light amber stringers for the broom bristles.

13. Add button details to the snowman with pieces of coarse black frit.

14. Medium black frit is used for the snowman's eyes and mouth.

15. Mix equal parts of white medium frit and clear iridized medium frit for snow. A small scoop or spoon will be helpful in placing frit onto the project.

16. To add a bit of color to the snow, sift a small amount of fine sky blue frit over the white and iridized clear snow mix. A powder sifter will help distribute the fine frit evenly.

17. A small spritz of hairspray will help hold the frit and design pieces in place.

18. Place the tile on a prepared kiln shelf that has been covered with a piece of thin kiln paper.

Carefully slide the kiln shelf into the kiln. Your snowman is ready to fire.

19. Use firing schedule A from page 34 or the firing guidelines below.

Firing Guidelines

Speed: Medium
Process: Tack Fuse
Top Temp: 1375°F
Hold Time: 12 Minutes

After firing, do not open the kiln until it has cooled to 100°F or less.

Pro Tip: Opening the door before the kiln and your project have cooled sufficiently may cause the glass to crack from thermal shock. Patience at this stage will be worth the extra time!

20. Your snowman tile is now complete. Carefully wash any kiln paper residue from the glass in your rinse basin. Allow the particles to settle, pour off the clear water, and dispose of the sediment in the trash bin.

There are many ways to use a tile like this snowman. I chose to incorporate this tile into a candleholder (using traditional stained glass methods).

MATERIALS FOR THE CANDLEHOLDER

- [ ] 1 mirror base (pattern on page 142)
- [ ] Four ³⁄₄ x 5-inch bevels
- [ ] Three 4 x 5-inch clear sides
- [ ] Fused snowman tile

Projects

Sometimes a sheet of glass is so beautiful that you can use it to make a great project without adding any other materials. This is especially true with Opal Art glass.

- Cutting Glass to Fit a Mold
- Firing Glass for a Smoother Edge
- Slumping Glass into a Mold

Projects

- [ ] Opal art glass: 1 square foot
  (this example uses Blackberry Cream)
- [ ] Prepared 9½-inch hexagon mold
- [ ] Ruler
- [ ] Glass marker
- [ ] Glass-cutting tools
- [ ] Thin kiln paper
- [ ] Prepared kiln shelf

1. As you look at your piece of glass, decide which section has the most exciting swirl pattern.

2. Turn the glass face down. The back of this glass is smoother, so we will be cutting the glass from this side for a more even score line.

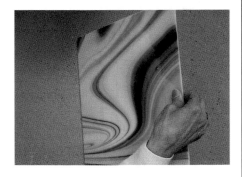

3. Position the hexagon mold, also facedown, over the section of glass you wish to highlight.

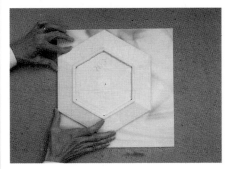

4. Use the glass marker to trace the shape of the plate mold onto the back of the glass.

5. Since the sides of your design are straight edges, you can use a ruler to help keep your cut lines straight. Place the ruler on the inside of the marker line to allow for the width of the cutter head. Score one side of the hexagon.

Break the glass along your score line.

Projects

6. Continue scoring and breaking the remaining sides of the hexagon.

Pro Tip: Take the time to fire your plate to a contour fuse before slumping it into the mold. This extra step will give your finished plate a nicely rounded edge. Note the difference between the edges of these two plates.

The plate on the top was slumped directly on the slumping mold. The plate on the bottom was fired twice: The first firing was to a contour fuse, and the second firing was to slump the glass on the mold. Notice how the edges of the second plate appear much smoother, giving it a more professional look.

7. Grind any rough edges with the glass turned facedown. This will help prevent chipping in the color swirl layer of the glass.

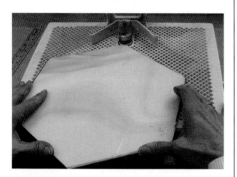

8. Wash, rinse, and dry the glass hexagon.

9. Place the glass on a prepared kiln shelf that has been covered with a sheet of thin kiln paper.

10. Use firing schedule B from page 34 or the firing guidelines below.

Firing Guidelines

Speed: Medium
Process: Contour Fuse
Top Temp: 1420°F
Hold Time: 12 Minutes

Allow the kiln to cool to 100°F or less. Carefully remove the glass from the kiln shelf and wash away any residue from the kiln paper. Allow the particles of debris to settle to the bottom of the rinse basin, pour off the clear water, and dispose of the sediment in the trash bin. Dry the glass thoroughly.

11. Remove the kiln shelf from the kiln and place the prepared hexagon mold on the kiln posts. This will allow any air between the glass and the mold to disperse through the vent holes in the mold. Position the glass over the mold.

Use firing schedule E from page 34 or the firing guidelines below.

Firing Guidelines

Speed: Slow
Process: Slump
Top Temp: 1250°F
Hold Time: 12 Minutes

Again, you must allow the kiln to cool to 100°F or less. Remove your finished plate from the mold and wash well.

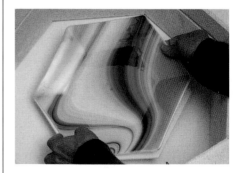

A set of plates like this can make a lovely table setting. Experiment with a variety of glass to complement your style.

You can create some very interesting projects using glass stringers and a few other components. One of the easiest projects to try is this votive cup. Experiment with different colors to reflect your taste.

- Using Glass Stringers
- Using a Spray Mold Release
- Draping Glass over a Mold

Projects

- [ ] Clear glass: $7^3/_4$-inch square
- [ ] Ruler
- [ ] 1 tube of deep aqua stringers
- [ ] $^1/_2$ tube of medium amber stringers
- [ ] 1 tube of clear stringers
- [ ] $^1/_2$ tube of dark green stringers
- [ ] Hairspray (pump container)
- [ ] Thin kiln paper
- [ ] Prepared kiln shelf
- [ ] Mold release
- [ ] Short floral former mold

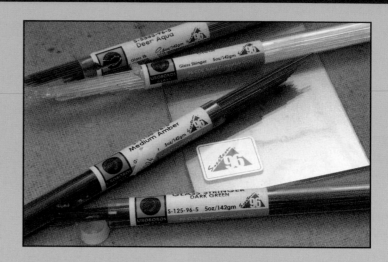

1. Place a sheet of thin kiln paper on your prepared kiln shelf.

2. Wash, rinse, and dry the clear square of glass and center it on the kiln paper.

3. Break stringers into $7^3/_4$-inch lengths with your fingers.

4. When you have plenty of stringers in each color, begin laying out the pattern. You will need about 60 deep aqua, 140 clear, 30 medium amber, and 30 dark green stringer segments for this votive cup.

5. Begin building the horizontal stringer layer about $^3/_4$ inch above the lower edge of the clear glass, keeping the stringer edges somewhat even with the sides of the glass.

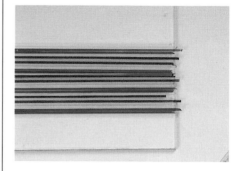

A small spritz of hairspray will keep the first few stringers from sliding out of position.

Projects

The sequence used in this sample is shown in the box below.

Stringer Sequence

2 deep aqua
2 clear
1 medium amber
1 clear
1 dark green
2 clear

6. Repeat this pattern across the square of glass until you are about ³/₄ inch from the top edge. Keep the stringers tightly together, but do not overlap. Try to end the sequence with two deep aqua stringers.

A small spritz of hairspray will keep this layer of stringers from shifting. Allow the spray to dry for a few minutes.

7. The vertical layer of stringers will begin about ³/₄ inch in from the right edge of your clear glass square. Begin with two deep aqua stringers and continue with the same sequence as before.

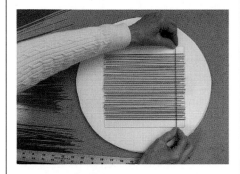

Once again, use a small spritz of hairspray to hold the first few stringers in position.

8. Continue building this top layer of stringers until you are about ³/₄ inch in from the left side of the glass square. Try to end the sequence with two deep aqua stringers. Use another small spritz of hairspray to hold the stringers in place.

9. You can add corner details by breaking some deep aqua and medium amber stringers into small segments. Here, I have centered an aqua stringer from the corner of the stringer sequences to the corner of the clear glass. I placed scraps of medium amber stringers to the left and right of the aqua segment and used a small spritz of hairspray to hold them in place.

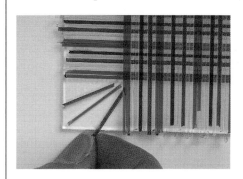

10. Repeat this design in the other three corners. The project is now ready to fire.

11. Carefully place the kiln shelf in the kiln and check that no stringers have shifted during the transfer from work table to kiln.

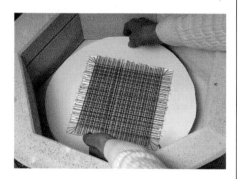

12. Use firing schedule A from page 34 or the following firing guidelines.

Firing Guidelines

Speed: Medium
Process: Tack Fuse
Top Temp: 1375°F
Hold Time: 12 Minutes

Do not open the kiln until the temperature has cooled to 100°F or less. At this temperature, you can safely remove the project from the kiln and clean off any residue from the kiln paper in your rinse basin. Dry the glass carefully.

13. Prepare a short floral former stainless steel mold by spraying it evenly with a mold release.

Allow the mold release to air-dry for a few minutes.

14. Mark the center of the closed end of the mold with your glass marker.

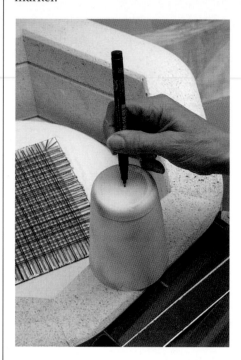

15. Cover the kiln shelf with a fresh piece of thin kiln paper, then position the mold on the shelf.

16. Measure the glass piece to locate the center and make a small dot with the glass marker. Center the glass over the mold, aligning the center of the glass with the center dot on the mold.

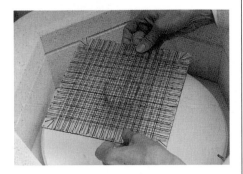

17. Use firing schedule E from page 34 or the firing guidelines below.

Firing Guidelines

Speed: Slow
Process: Slump
Top Temp: 1250°F
Hold Time: 12 Minutes

Again, allow the kiln to cool to 100°F or less before you open it. Carefully remove the glass from the mold.

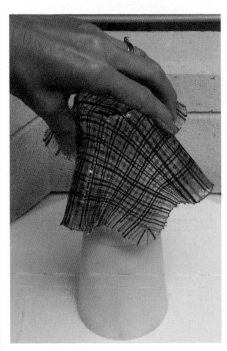

18. Wash and dry the votive cup, add your favorite candle, and your stringer project is ready to enjoy!

Another project you can make using stringers is this delicate stringer bowl. Because it does not have a clear base glass, this bowl is more fragile, but very beautiful.

- Making a Bowl
- Building a Project Directly on the Kiln Shelf

MATERIALS

- [ ] 1 tube of dark green stringers
- [ ] ½ tube of cherry red stringers
- [ ] 1 tube of clear stringers
- [ ] ½ tube of white opal stringers
- [ ] Ruler
- [ ] Hairspray (pump container)
- [ ] Thin kiln paper
- [ ] Prepared kiln shelf
- [ ] Prepared mold, 8½-inch square

1. Begin by drawing an 8½-inch square on the kiln paper, then place the paper on the prepared kiln shelf.

2. Break the stringers into 8½-inch lengths with your fingers. Continue until you have enough stringers to begin laying out the pattern. A bowl of this size will use about 120 dark green, 120 clear, 30 cherry red, and 30 white opal stringer segments.

3. Start the sequence by placing two dark green stringers about ¾ inch from the lower edge of the square that you drew on the kiln paper. A small spritz of hairspray will help to keep the stringers in place.

The stringer sequence used in this sample is shown below.

Stringer Sequence

2 dark green
1 clear
2 dark green
1 clear
1 cherry red
1 clear
1 white opal
1 clear

4. Continue building your plate by following the sequence, keeping the stringers close together.

5. End this stringer layer about ¾ inch from the top edge of the square drawn on the kiln paper, finishing the pattern with two dark green stringers.

6. Spray lightly with the hairspray and allow the project to air-dry for a few minutes.

7. Begin building the vertical layer of stringers about ¾ inch from the right side of the square. Once again, that small spritz of hairspray will help to keep the stringers in place.

8. Continue the pattern sequence. Notice that the stringer ends are close to the edges of the square, but not exactly even. This will give a ruffled look to the edges of your bowl.

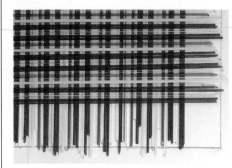

9. Place the remainder of the vertical layer of stringers, ending with two dark green stringers about ¾ inch from the left edge of the square.

10. Spritz with the hairspray and allow the project to air-dry for a few minutes.

11. Carefully move the kiln shelf into the kiln and check to see that the stringers have not shifted.

12. Use firing schedule A from page 34 or the firing guidelines below.

Firing Guidelines

Speed: Medium
Process: Tack Fuse
Top Temp: 1375°F
Hold Time: 12 Minutes

13. Allow the kiln to cool to 100°F or less before opening the lid. Gently remove the glass from the kiln shelf and remove any kiln paper residue by dipping the glass in your rinse basin. Dry the glass gently.

14. Remove the shelf from the kiln and set aside. Position the kiln posts to support your square slumping mold.

Projects

15. Place the fired stringer piece over the mold.

16. Use firing schedule E from page 34 or the firing guidelines below.

Firing Guidelines

Speed: Slow
Process: Slump
Top Temp: 1250°F
Hold Time: 12 Minutes

When the kiln has cooled to 100°F or less, you can remove your finished stringer bowl.

This design can be made in any color combination to complement your décor.

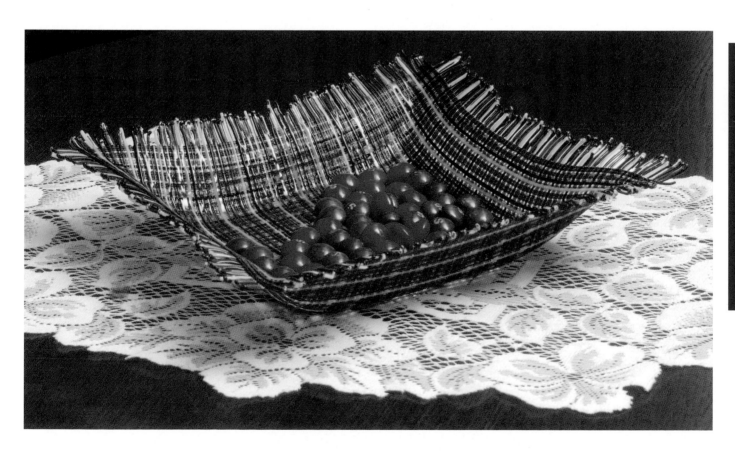

Projects

Here is a fun project to bring some holiday cheer into your home. Hang your chimes where a slight breeze will sway the glass trees. Note: In cold climates, this project is best for indoor use only.

The pattern can be found on page 143.

- Using Fusing Wire
- Using Frit
- Assembling a Wind Chime

- [ ] Sea green glass: $\frac{1}{4}$ square foot
- [ ] Light green glass: $\frac{1}{4}$ square foot
- [ ] Dark green glass: $\frac{1}{4}$ square foot
- [ ] Bronze glass: $\frac{1}{4}$ square foot
- [ ] Yellow opal glass: $\frac{1}{4}$ square foot
- [ ] White opal medium frit
- [ ] Pattern templates
- [ ] Glass marker
- [ ] Fusing wire (24 gauge)
- [ ] Wire cutters
- [ ] Glass cutting tools
- [ ] Hairspray (pump container)
- [ ] Ruler
- [ ] Wooden skewer
- [ ] Prepared kiln shelf
- [ ] Thin kiln paper

MAKING THE WIND CHIME PIECES

Materials for assembling the wind chime will be listed later.

1. For each of the five trees, you will need one small, one medium, and one large piece of green glass. Trace around the pattern templates with the glass marker.

2. Cut out each tree section, a total of fifteen pieces.

3. Cut five strips of bronze glass using the template for the tree trunks. Finally, cut the five star points and the center from the yellow opal glass.

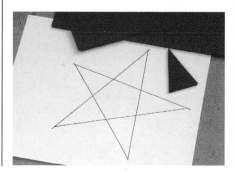

4. Use the grinder to smooth the edges of the glass pieces.

5. Wash, rinse, and dry all glass pieces.

Projects

6. Cut six pieces of fusing wire into 1-inch lengths.

7. Bend each segment of wire over the wooden skewer to give it a nicely rounded top.

8. Place a sheet of thin kiln paper on your prepared kiln shelf. Arrange the five yellow star points with their inner edges touching.

9. Position the center of the star over the star points, making sure the inner edges of the points are covered.

10. Place a hook at the top of one star point.

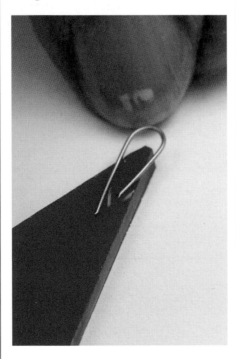

11. Use a scrap of the yellow glass to make a small triangle to cover the hook.

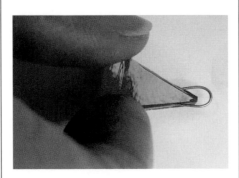

A wooden skewer can be helpful for moving small pieces of glass into position.

12. Place one of the bronze strips of glass on your kiln paper. Add a hook at the top of the bronze strip and place a small tree section over the hook. Now place a medium tree section on the bronze strip with the top point overlapping the bottom of the small tree section.

13. Position the large tree section on the same bronze strip so that it overlaps the bottom of the medium tree section.

14. Lay out the remaining four trees, making sure there is at least a ½-inch space between all the trees. A small spritz of hairspray will help to keep glass pieces in place.

15. While the hairspray is still damp, sprinkle white opal frit on each tree to give it a snowy look.

16. Carefully place the kiln shelf in the kiln and check that no components have shifted during the transfer from work table to kiln.

Pro Tip: The glass has pulled in at the edges because I fired single layers of glass to a full fuse temperature. For the wind chime, this is the look I was hoping to get, but a similar look in a tile would not be optimal. For a tile, you would want to add an additional layer of base glass or lower your firing temperature to the tack fuse range.

17. Use firing schedule C from page 34 or the firing guidelines below.

Firing Guidelines

Speed: Medium
Process: Full Fuse
Top Temp: 1480°F
Hold Time: 12 Minutes

18. After firing, allow the kiln to cool to 100°F or less before you open it. Here is how your trees and star will appear after firing:

Remove the fired glass from the kiln shelf. You can see here that kiln paper residue is lifting off the shelf as well.

19. Wash away the kiln paper residue in a basin of water, allow the particles to settle on the bottom of the basin, and pour off the clear water. The sediment should be discarded in the trash bin.

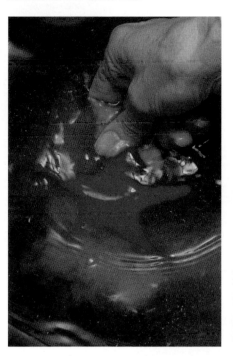

63

Projects

Dry the glass carefully with a towel.

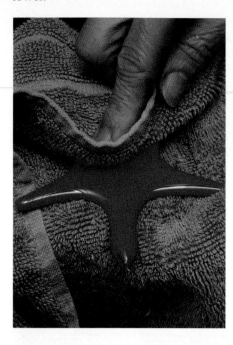

20. Dispose of the fired kiln paper that remains on the shelf by sliding it into your trash bin. Wear a dust mask for protection against airborne particles.

MATERIALS

☐ 5 fused trees

☐ 1 fused star

☐ 13 red beads

☐ 13 clear beads

☐ Bead stringing wire, 0.015 inch in diameter

☐ Scissors

☐ 6-inch metal star (available at craft stores)

☐ Crimp beads

☐ Crimping pliers

ASSEMBLING THE WIND CHIME

1. Run a strand of the bead wire through the center hole of the star to create a hanging loop.

2. Slide one crimp bead, one red bead, one clear bead, and another crimp bead onto the bead wire.

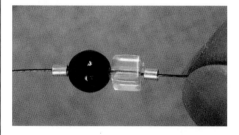

3. Run one end of the bead wire back through those same beads.

4. Leave a large loop in the bead wire.

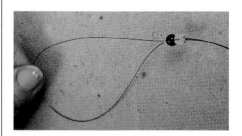

5. Use the crimping pliers to squeeze the lower crimp bead tight to the bead wire.

6. Do the same with the top crimp bead. Give the beads a gentle tug to make sure they are securely fastened to the bead wire.

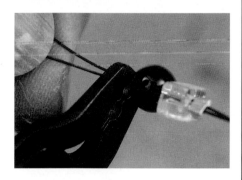

7. String the loose end of the bead wire back through the center of the star, pulling the bead sequence snug against the top of the star.

8. Leave an 8-inch length of bead wire extending from the bottom of the metal star and trim with scissors. Slide one clear bead, one red bead, and one crimp bead up the 8-inch length of wire. Make sure the short tail of the bead wire is also covered by the beads. Squeeze the crimp bead with the crimping pliers. The star will be added to the bottom of this wire later.

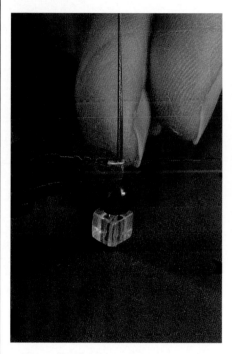

9. It is time to add the trees to the wind chime. At one of the metal star points, thread a piece of bead wire up through one hole and down through an adjacent hole.

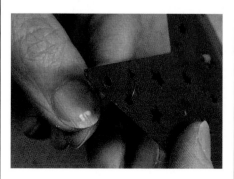

10. Slide one clear bead, one red bead, and one crimp bead onto the bead wire. Squeeze the crimp bead with the crimping pliers after checking that both the long and short ends of the bead wire have gone through the holes in the beads.

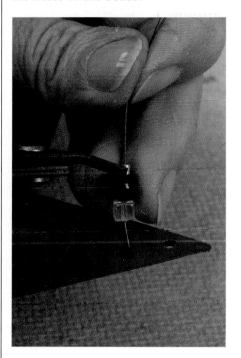

11. Cut the long end of the bead wire to about 6 inches. String on one crimp bead, one red bead, and one clear bead, then slip the strand through the hook of one of the trees.

12. Run that strand of bead wire back through the bead sequence, and squeeze the crimp bead with the crimping pliers.

Gently tug on the tree to make sure the crimp beads are tight and the glass piece is secure.

13. Continue stringing the remaining trees in the same manner. The trees should all hang at an even length from the metal star.

14. Finally, we will add the yellow star to create the chime. Take the bead wire hanging from the center of the metal star, and slide on one crimp bead, one red bead, and one clear bead. Then take the wire through the hook of the yellow star. Adjust the height of the yellow star so the points can gently brush against the trees. Run the bead wire strand back through the bead sequence and squeeze the crimp bead with the crimping pliers.

This project took a lot of time and work to assemble, but the end result is a great holiday project.

Hang your wind chimes in a favorite spot, but remember to enjoy them indoors.

Embossing is a great way to add a relief design in glass. The ornaments made here are for Easter, but the technique can be adapted for any holiday season. For best results, use light shades of cathedral (transparent) glass.

The pattern can be found on page 143.

- Using Fiber Paper
- Using Fusing Wire
- Firing Two Layers of Glass for a Smooth Edge

Projects

- [ ] ¹⁄₁₆-inch thick fiber paper
- [ ] Craft knife
- [ ] 24-gauge fusing wire
- [ ] Wire cutters
- [ ] Decorative paper punches
- [ ] Glass marker
- [ ] Clear glass
- [ ] Light colors of cathedral glass
- [ ] Oval pattern templates
- [ ] Glass-cutting tools
- [ ] Prepared kiln shelf
- [ ] Thin kiln paper

Projects

1. Trace around the template marked "clear" on the clear glass. You will need a clear oval for each ornament you wish to make.

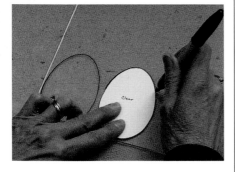

2. Trace around the template marked "color" on several different pieces of colored glass.

3. Cut out all ovals, both clear and colored.

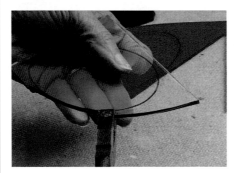

4. Grind all oval pieces to smooth the edges.

Pro Tip: You will notice that the clear ovals are just slightly larger than the colored ovals. The clear glass will be the top layer of your ornaments. During the fusing process, that extra bit of clear glass will melt over the edges of the colored glass, giving the ornaments a smooth, finished look.

5. Wash, rinse, and dry all glass pieces.

6. Place a sheet of thin kiln paper on your prepared kiln shelf.

7. Trace the "color" template on the kiln paper for each ornament you are making. Allow at least $1/2$ inch of space between all the shapes.

8. Use the decorative paper punches to cut butterfly shapes and bunny shapes from the $1/16$-inch fiber paper.

9. You can also use a regular hole punch to make circles, or cut wavy stripes, grass, or other shapes from the paper with a craft knife.

10. Position these fiber paper designs inside the traced oval shapes, arranging them to make your own unique designs.

11. Cover the fiber paper designs with colored glass ovals. It is okay if some of the fiber paper extends beyond the edge of the colored glass.

12. You will need to add a hook to each egg for hanging the ornaments. Cut 1-inch lengths of 24-gauge fusing wire.

13. Fold each wire in half. A wooden skewer can make the folding easier.

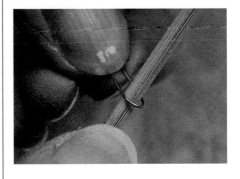

14. Add a hook at the top of each colored glass ornament on the kiln shelf.

Projects

15. Cover each ornament with a clear glass oval.

16. Carefully slide the kiln shelf of Easter ornaments into the kiln.

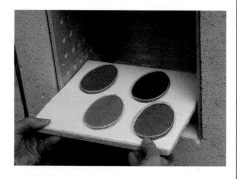

17. Adjust any glass pieces that may have shifted during the transfer from work table to kiln.

18. Use firing schedule D from page 34 or the firing guidelines below. We will fire the ornaments at a slow speed to prevent bubbles from forming between the glass layers.

Firing Guidelines

Speed: Slow
Process: Full Fuse
Top Temp: 1480°F
Hold Time: 12 Minutes

19. After the firing process is complete, allow the kiln to cool to 100°F or less.

Your finished ornaments will look similar to these.

Gently lift the ornaments from the kiln paper.

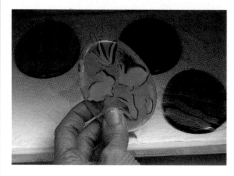

20. Use your craft knife to carefully remove the fiber paper designs from the ornaments.

Pro Tip: Fiber paper designs can be reused to make more ornaments if they are in good condition. With each firing, the fiber paper will become softer, so remove it from the ornaments very gently.

21. Wash, rinse, and dry the ornaments. Remember to carefully dispose of any kiln paper or fiber paper residue.

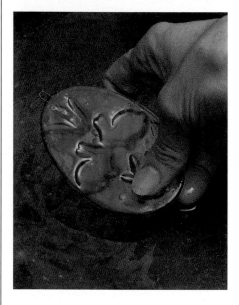

Add a colorful ribbon through the hook of each ornament to display them during the holiday season.

Projects

The same embossing technique shown in the Easter Ornament project can be used to create a beautiful plate. For this project, we will use 1/8-inch fiber paper to create a deeper impression in the glass. You will obtain the best results when using lighter shades of cathedral (transparent) glass.

The pattern can be found on page 144.

- Transferring a Pattern
- Using Fiber Paper
- Slumping Glass over a Mold

Projects

☐ Light blue cathedral glass: $8^1/_2$-inch square

☐ Pattern

☐ Clear glass: $8^7/_{16}$-inch square

☐ Fine-tipped pen

☐ 8-inch square of $^1/_8$-inch fiber paper

☐ Craft knife

☐ Carbon paper

☐ Masking tape

☐ Small ruler

☐ Prepared kiln shelf

☐ Thin kiln paper

☐ Prepared $8^1/_2$-inch square slumping mold

1. Begin by placing an 8-inch square of carbon paper over the fiber paper and covering it with the pattern.

2. Tape the edges of this packet with masking tape to prevent the pattern from shifting.

3. Using the fine-tipped pen and the ruler, trace over the pattern design.

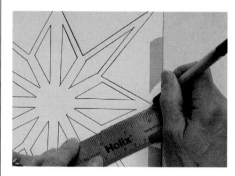

4. Remove the tape and separate the fiber paper from the carbon and pattern papers.

5. Use a craft knife and the ruler to cut the exterior lines of the design.

6. Cut along the interior lines of the design and remove the pieces of fiber paper.

Projects

When finished, the fiber paper looks like this.

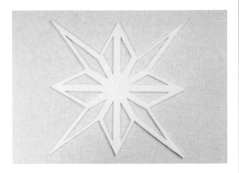

7. Wash, rinse, and dry the light blue and clear glass squares.

8. On the prepared kiln shelf, place a sheet of thin kiln paper. Position the fiber paper design in the center of the kiln shelf.

9. Center the light blue glass over the fiber paper design.

Pro Tip: When you fire two full pieces of glass, the top layer of glass should always be slightly larger than the base glass. When fired to a full fuse, the extra glass melts gently over the base layer to form a smooth edge on the finished project.

10. Now place the clear glass square over the light blue piece.

11. Use firing schedule D from page 34 or the firing guidelines below.

Firing Guidelines

Speed: Slow
Process: Full Fuse
Top Temp: 1480°F
Hold Time: 12 Minutes

12. After firing, allow the kiln and your project to cool to 100°F or less before removing your glass.

13. When you slump your plate, the fiber paper must remain in place to keep the design as deep as possible. This photo shows the reverse side of the glass with the fiber paper in place.

Remove the shelf from the kiln and center your square slumping mold over the kiln posts. This will allow any air between the glass and the mold to escape through the vent holes in the mold. Center the glass with the fiber paper side down, over the slumping mold.

14. Use firing schedule E from page 34 or the firing guidelines below.

Firing Guidelines

Speed: Slow
Process: Slump
Top Temp: 1250°F
Hold Time: 12 Minutes

Projects

15. When the kiln has cooled to 100°F or less, you can remove your finished plate.

Note: If you carefully remove the fiber paper design, you will be able to reuse it in additional firings.

Gently wash away any fiber paper or kiln paper residue from your project.

This plate is great for serving cookies or pastries!

This pocket vase is a sweet way to hang a few flowers on your wall. We've made a small version, but the concept can be used on any scale. If you choose to make a larger pocket vase, you will want to use several layers of the fiber paper to create a larger space for flower stems.

The pattern can be found on page 145.

- Using Glass Nuggets
- Using Fiber Paper
- Drilling Holes in Glass

Projects

75

- [ ] Clear fusible glass
- [ ] Leaves cut from a variety of green glass shades
- [ ] Tiny nuggets
- [ ] Bent green stringers
- [ ] Pattern
- [ ] Glass-cutting tools
- [ ] 1/8-inch fiber paper
- [ ] Prepared kiln shelf
- [ ] Thin kiln paper

1. Cut the clear fusing glass according to the pattern. Wash, rinse, and dry the glass pieces.

2. The shorter piece of glass will be the top of your pocket vase. Place a few leaves in various shades of green on this piece of glass.

3. Create flowers using small fused nuggets made from scrap glass. Use different colored nuggets for the flower centers. See Chapter 2, Preparing Accent Components, for instructions for making your own nuggets and bent stringers.

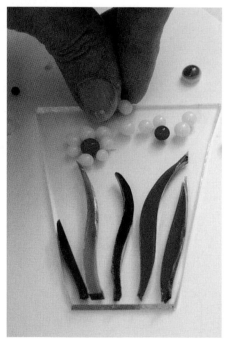

4. Add a couple of gently bent stringers for flower stems.

5. Fire the pocket vase top glass on your prepared kiln shelf covered with a sheet of thin kiln paper. This project is sharing the kiln space with another project that will be fired to the same temperature.

Use firing schedule A from page 34 or the firing guidelines below.

6. When the kiln has cooled to 100°F or less, you can remove your glass and wash away any kiln paper residue.

The components are now ready to assemble into the pocket vase.

7. Place the pocket vase base on a prepared kiln shelf covered with a sheet of thin kiln paper. Cut two pieces of thin kiln paper and a 1/8-inch piece of fiber paper as indicated on the pattern sheet. Position one of the pieces of kiln paper, smooth side down, on the base glass.

8. Lay the fiber paper directly on the kiln paper and place the second kiln paper piece over that, with the smooth side up.

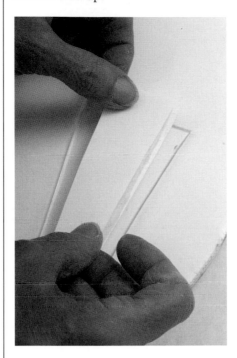

9. Center the fired top piece of glass over the top of the whole thing, and you are ready for your second firing.

10. Use firing schedule A from page 34 or the firing guidelines below. This is the same tack fuse program that was used to fuse the design pieces to the top glass.

11. After firing, remove the pocket vase from the kiln when it has cooled to 100°F or less. Carefully remove the fiber paper and kiln paper from the pocket they have formed. Remember to handle these products with care, and wear your dust mask.

Projects

- ☐ Bowl
- ☐ Glass scrap
- ☐ Thin packing foam
- ☐ Water
- ☐ Glass marker
- ☐ Petroleum jelly
- ☐ High-speed drill with 1 mm diamond bit
- ☐ Twisted colored wire

The best way to display your pocket vase is to add a decorative wire loop for hanging it. To attach this wire, you will need to drill two small holes in the base glass layer. Drilling holes in glass requires a special technique so that the heat generated by the drill bit does not crack the glass.

1. Use the glass marker to make a tiny dot in each top corner of the base glass of the pocket vase.

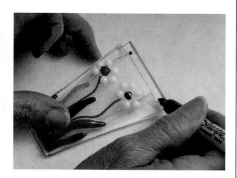

2. A smudge of petroleum jelly will keep the marker from washing away in the water.

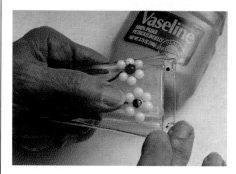

3. Place the glass scrap in the bowl, then the thin packing foam, and place your pocket vase on top.

4. Add water until it barely covers the marker dots.

5. Turn the drill to its highest speed and place it against one of the marker dots. Allow the drill bit to grind easily through the glass rather than applying forceful pressure. Drill another hole at the other marker dot.

6. After both holes have been drilled, wipe away the petroleum jelly residue with a paper towel.

7. Thread one end of the twisted wire up through one of the drilled holes and wrap it around itself to hold it in place.

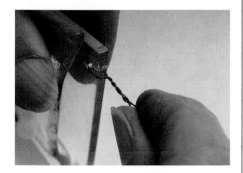

8. Thread the opposite end of the twisted wire up through the remaining hole. Trim the wire to an appropriate length and twist the end to the main wire to form a loop.

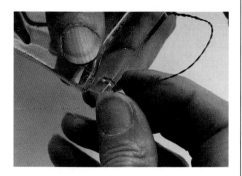

Your pocket vase is ready to hang and fill with flowers!

Working with dichroic glass is a lot of fun. The extra shimmer found in this glass makes it perfect for small projects like jewelry, wine bottle stoppers, and drawer pulls. These projects will use the same firing schedule, allowing you to maximize the use of your kiln space. Make as many projects as will fit comfortably on the kiln shelf and fire them together.

The patterns for the projects made here can be found on page 146.

- Using Dichroic Glass
- Using Dichro Slide Paper
- Attching Glass to Metal Findings

Projects

MATERIALS

- ☐ Thin clear fusible glass
- ☐ Thin black fusible glass
- ☐ Variety of dichroic glass pieces
- ☐ Dichro Slide paper
- ☐ Decorative paper punches
- ☐ Earring bails
- ☐ Pendant bails
- ☐ Wine bottle stopper
- ☐ Drawer pull
- ☐ Black glass marker
- ☐ Silver glass marker
- ☐ Shallow plate
- ☐ Distilled water
- ☐ Paper towels
- ☐ Glass-cutting tools
- ☐ Artist's brayer
- ☐ E6000 adhesive
- ☐ Thin kiln paper
- ☐ Prepared kiln shelf

Note: Wash, rinse, and dry all glass before you assemble the projects.

SIMPLE PENDANT

1. The first piece is a pendant featuring Dichro Slide paper. This material is made like a decal, with a dichroic coating and a protective paper backing. Use a decorative paper punch to cut a design from the Dichro Slide paper.

2. Pour a small amount of distilled water into the shallow plate.

3. Soak the cut design in the water for a minute or so, just until the paper backing begins to slip free from the decal.

Projects

4. Position the cut decal onto a 1 by 1½-inch thin black glass rectangle.

5. Gently slide the protective paper from beneath the decal layer.

6. Blot away the excess water with a paper towel.

7. Burnish the dichroic decal to the black glass with a clean brayer.

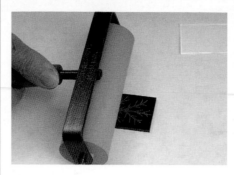

Pro Tip: Covering dichroic glass with a clear cap will magnify the dichroic shimmer. Just a little bit of dichroic glass can wow you with its effect!

8. Allow the piece to air-dry, then cap with a rectangle of thin clear glass 1¹⁄₁₆ by 1⁹⁄₁₆ inches.

EARRINGS

1. Patterned dichroic glass can be used to make a small pair of earrings. Cut ½-inch strips from the patterned glass.

2. Score each strip into ½-inch sections and separate the pieces.

3. Cover each design square with a ⁹⁄₁₆-inch cap of thin clear glass.

Some smaller earring pieces will also be included in this firing. These are ¼-inch squares of dichroic glass which have been capped with ⁵⁄₁₆-inch squares of thin clear glass.

SHAPED PENDANT

1. This pendant is made with a thin black base, a design layer cut from dichroic glass, and then a top cap of thin clear glass. Trace the leaf-shaped pattern marked "black" onto thin black glass with a silver marker.

2. Trace the leaf-shaped pattern marked "clear" onto the thin clear glass with the black marker.

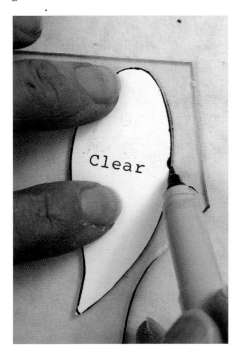

3. Cut out the glass pieces, grind to smooth any rough edges, and clean the glass well. Cut any design you like from your dichroic glass.

Pro Tip: Always cut dichroic glass on the non-coated side to prevent chipping. To determine which side of the glass has the coating, scratch it gently with a fingernail. The side that produces a scratchy sound has the dichroic coating.

When putting the clear glass cap on a jewelry piece, it is important to have a design that is balanced. The small side pieces in this design are a little thicker due to their texture. The clear cap has been balanced by adding these pieces on either side of the center design glass.

WINE BOTTLE STOPPERS AND DRAWER PULLS

1. You can cut out several wine bottle stoppers and drawer pulls at the same time. Each piece will require a black or dark base and a clear glass cap. Use the silver marker to trace the templates marked "black" onto thin black glass.

2. Use the black marker to trace the templates labeled "clear" onto thin clear glass.

3. Cut out the glass pieces and grind any rough edges.

4. Wash, rinse, and dry all glass pieces prior to assembly.

Note: Save all dichroic glass scraps. Even the tiniest bit of dichroic can be used on these small projects.

5. Cut the dichroic glass into any shape you like, and place the pieces on a black base.

6. Cover the design layer with a cap of thin clear glass, making sure the cap is balanced over the design layer.

7. Place all pieces to be fired on a prepared kiln shelf covered with a sheet of thin kiln paper. As you can see, I have a large variety of projects here that will be fired to a full fuse.

8. Use firing schedule D from page 34 or the firing guidelines below. Using a slow speed to fire these projects will help prevent air bubbles from forming around the dichroic glass.

Firing Guidelines

Speed: Slow
Process: Full Fuse
Top Temp: 1480°F
Hold Time: 12 Minutes

After the kiln has cooled to 100° or less, you may remove your projects. Be sure to wash away any kiln paper residue from the back of your glass pieces. Dry the glass thoroughly.

Projects

MOUNTING JEWELRY CABOCHONS

1. I use E6000 adhesive to adhere a bail to each pendant piece. To do this, simply squeeze a small amount of the adhesive into the depression of the bail.

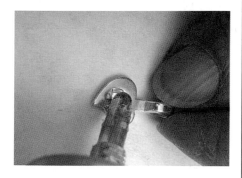

2. Center the pendant cabochon over the bail and press firmly.

3. For the earrings, use a pair of needle-nose pliers to open the loop of an earring wire.

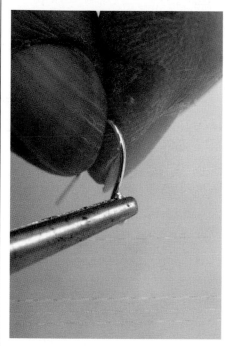

4. Slip the earring bail over the loop.

5. Close the loop with the needle-nose pliers.

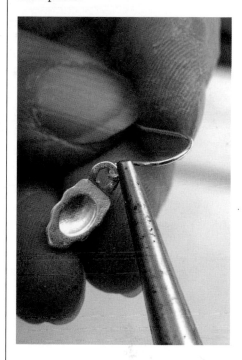

6. Place a small amount of adhesive in the depression of the bail and press the dichroic cabochon into place.

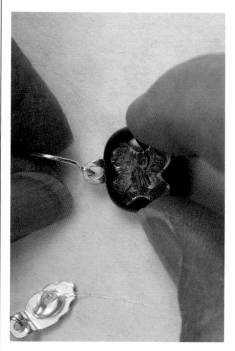

7. The finished pendants and earrings should be placed on a flat surface for at least 24 hours to allow the adhesive to set.

MOUNTING WINE BOTTLE STOPPERS AND DRAWER PULLS

1. You can use the same adhesive to attach the cabochon to the wine bottle stopper. Make a serpentine shape with the adhesive on the back of the glass.

2. Press the glass firmly onto the wine bottle stopper.

3. The drawer pull will be assembled in the same manner. Put the adhesive on the back of the glass cabochon.

4. Press the glass firmly into the cup of the drawer pull.

5. Place these pieces on a flat surface and allow the adhesive to cure for at least 24 hours.

Your dichroic glass pieces are now ready to accent your home—and they make great gifts, too!

Stamping on glass with enamel is a great way to give fused glass a different look. You can make any kind of design on the glass by varying the type of stamps you use. Rubber stamps from the craft store come in many different designs to make one-of-a-kind projects.

- Using Glass Enamels
- Stamping Techniques
- Posting to Avoid Air Bubbles

Projects

- ☐ Opal orange glass: two 4¼-inch squares
- ☐ Sunflower yellow glass: two 4¼-inch squares
- ☐ Clear glass: one 8⁹⁄₁₆-inch square
- ☐ Clear stringer
- ☐ Rubber stamps with fern and leaf designs
- ☐ Black enamel powder
- ☐ Fuse Master Fusing Solution
- ☐ Scrap glass to use as a palette
- ☐ Small palette knife
- ☐ Artist's brayer
- ☐ Dust mask
- ☐ Prepared 8½-inch slumping mold
- ☐ Thin kiln paper
- ☐ Prepared kiln shelf

Note: Some enamels contain lead and will not be considered food-safe unless capped with a clear piece of glass. Read the labels carefully when using these products. Always handle enamel with care and wear a dust mask for protection.

1. Wash, rinse, and thoroughly dry all glass pieces.

2. Lay out the orange and yellow glass squares in an alternating color pattern, keeping the squares close together.

3. Sprinkle a small amount of black enamel on the glass palette.

4. Squeeze some of the fusing solution onto the black enamel.

5. Use the palette knife to blend the solution into the enamel.

6. Roll the brayer through the mixture until it becomes a thin layer.

7. Gently press a rubber stamp into the enamel mixture.

8. The design side of the stamp should have a uniform layer of the enamel mixture on it.

9. Press the stamp straight down onto one of the glass squares.

10. Continue pressing the stamps into the enamel mixture and onto the glass.

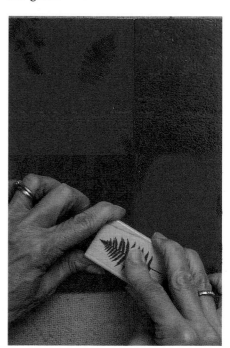

Projects

11. Stamp some designs over the seams between the glass squares.

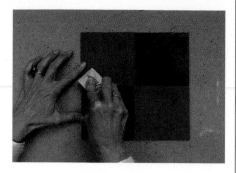

12. Stamp a few partial designs at the outer edges of the glass.

13. Allow the enamel to air-dry overnight.

14. Cover the kiln shelf with a sheet of thin kiln paper and reassemble the four squares of glass on it.

Pro Tip: Smart fusers will maximize their kiln space whenever possible. I have prepared four additional tiles that will use the same firing program as this enamel plate.

15. In this project, the two large pieces of glass are nearly identical in size. When two pieces of glass the same size are fused together, air bubbles can get trapped between the layers of glass. You can use a technique called posting to avoid this. Using your grozing pliers, nip a clear stringer into several ⅛-inch lengths.

16. Position a clear stringer segment at each of the four corners of the stamped plate, and place one near the midpoint of each side.

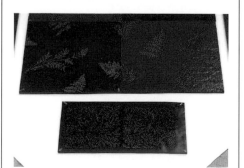

17. Center the clear glass square over the four colored squares.

18. The four rectangular tiles have also been covered with clear glass caps.

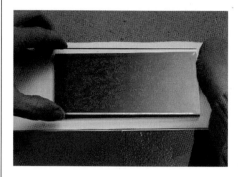

Notice the stringer segment between the clear and colored layers of glass. This space will allow air to escape before the edges of the glass fuse together.

19. Carefully place the kiln shelf in the kiln and check to make sure no glass has shifted.

20. Use firing schedule D from page 34 or the firing guidelines below.

Firing Guidelines

Speed: Slow
Process: Full Fuse
Top Temp: 1480°F
Hold Time: 12 Minutes

21. After firing, allow the kiln to cool to 100°F or less before opening the lid. Remove your fired plate and the four tiles.

22. Remove the kiln shelf from the kiln and position an 8 ½-inch square slumping mold on the kiln posts.

23. Center the stamped plate over the slumping mold.

24. Use firing schedule E from page 34 or the firing guidelines below.

Firing Guidelines

Speed: Slow
Process: Slump
Top Temp: 1250°F
Hold Time: 12 Minutes

25. Again, the kiln must cool down to 100°F or less before you open it. Remove your slumped plate from the mold and wash well to remove any residue from the kiln paper.

Your stamped plate will be a great addition to a fall-themed table setting, while the stamped tiles can be used as part of a tiled wall or backsplash, or as trivets.

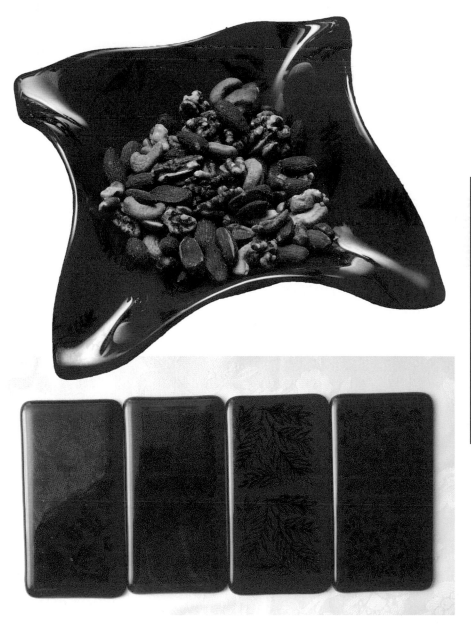

This project uses a photo fusing technique to transfer an image onto glass. Black and white photos or text can be made into a decal that will endure the heat of your kiln and turn into a soft sepia-toned image when fired. The design possibilities for this process are endless.

Preparing a decal for the photo fusing process is not difficult but does require special attention to the necessary equipment.

When choosing a photo for your project, look for a black and white picture with good contrast in the gray tones. Scan or import the photo into your computer.

To print a decal for the photo fusing process, it is important to choose a black and white laser printer that has a high concentration of iron oxide in the toner. HP black and white printers with genuine HP toner cartridges are essential for the photo fusing process. The printer used in this project was an HP Laser-Jet P1505n.

Warm up the printer by printing six to eight copies of your photo on plain paper. You will need to know which side of the paper your printer is printing on. Hand feed one piece of the photo fuse decal paper into your printer so that the photo will print on the glossy side.

Photo fuse decals can also be printed with black text. Simply type the text on your computer's word processing program, format it to your liking, and follow the steps above to print on the special photo fuse decal paper. Look for this paper at stained glass stores and online suppliers that carry glass fusing supplies.

- Preparing a Photo Fuse Decal
- Transferring Decals to Glass
- Using Glass Stringers

Projects

- ☐ White opal glass: 8½-inch square
- ☐ Black stringers
- ☐ Black glass: four 7¹⁵⁄₁₆-by-½-inch strips
- ☐ Prepared photo fuse decal
- ☐ Scissors
- ☐ Artist's brayer
- ☐ Distilled water
- ☐ Shallow plate
- ☐ Prepared kiln shelf
- ☐ Thin kiln paper
- ☐ Prepared 8½-inch square slumping mold
- ☐ Ruler
- ☐ Paper towels

1. Wash, rinse, and dry all glass pieces for this project.

2. Assemble the black strips at the top, bottom, and two sides of the white base glass to form a border.

3. Use scissors to trim the photo decal close to the printed image. Place the decal face down in a shallow plate of distilled water.

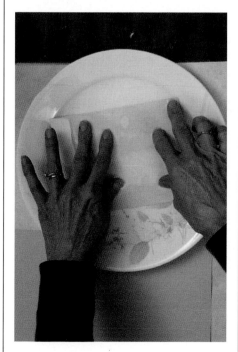

4. Soak the decal for 1½ to 2 minutes. Feel the edge of the decal to see if the image is ready to slide off the protective paper backing.

Projects

5. Hold the left edge of the decal against the white glass and slide the paper backing away.

6. Position the decal on the glass and smooth out any wrinkles.

7. Use a ruler to make sure the decal is centered on the glass.

8. Blot any excess water away with a paper towel.

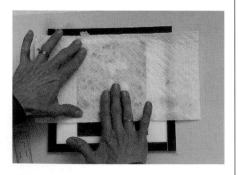

9. Remove one or two of the black border strips so you can smooth the decal using a clean artist's brayer.

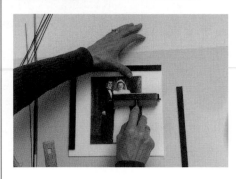

10. Blot again with a paper towel to remove any additional moisture. Reposition the black border strips at the edges of the base glass.

11. To make an inner border, break black stringers to the dimensions of your photo decal.

12. Position the stringer pieces around the perimeter of the photo decal.

13. Allow the photo decal to air-dry overnight. The project will then be ready for the first firing.

14. Place the project on a prepared kiln shelf that has been covered with thin kiln paper and carefully put the shelf in the kiln.

Projects

15. Take a moment to check the alignment of the black stringers and border pieces.

16. Use firing schedule B from page 34 or the firing guidelines below.

Firing Guidelines

Speed: Medium
Process: Contour Fuse
Top Temp: 1420°F
Hold Time: 12 Minutes

17. When the firing is complete and the kiln temperature has cooled to 100°F or less, remove your project from the kiln. Note that the photo decal has lightened in color to a beautiful sepia tone.

18. Remove the kiln shelf from the kiln and place your slumping mold on the kiln posts.

19. Position the project over the mold in preparation for the slump firing.

20. Use firing schedule E from page 34 or the firing guidelines below.

Firing Guidelines

Speed: Slow
Process: Slump
Top Temp: 1250°F
Hold Time: 12 Minutes

21. When the slump firing is complete and the temperature of the kiln has cooled to 100°F or less, remove the glass from the kiln.

Wash the project gently to remove any kiln wash or kiln paper residue.

A plate like this makes a lovely gift that will be treasured for many years.

You can use the same photo fusing process shown in the Heirloom Photo Plate to add text to a fusing project. Here, we have chosen text to commemorate a special occasion.

The pattern can be found on page 147.

- Preparing a Pattern
- Using Color Variations in Glass

1. Lay out the papers with the oak tag on the bottom, the carbon paper in the center, and the tracing paper on top. Tape the edges of the paper packet to your work table with masking tape to keep the papers from sliding out of position.

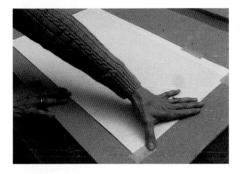

MATERIALS FOR PATTERN PREPARATION

☐ Oak tag
☐ Carbon paper
☐ Tracing paper
☐ Masking tape
☐ Pencil
☐ Compass
☐ Pattern
☐ Scissors

2. Use a compass to draw a circle 11½ inches in diameter on the paper packet.

3. Slide the calla lily pattern between the tracing paper and the carbon paper.

4. Position the design within the circle you just drew.

5. Tape the pattern securely in place.

6. Trace the design, pressing hard enough with your pencil to transfer the design to the oak tag on the bottom of the packet.

7. Number the pattern pieces.

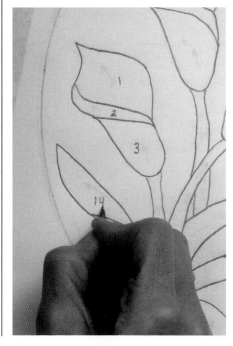

97

Projects

8. Add arrows to indicate the direction of the color grain in the glass.

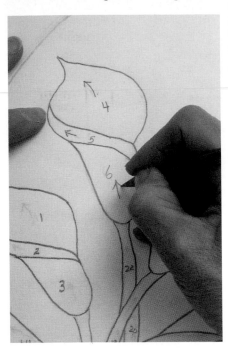

9. Use a color code to mark the pattern with your glass color choices.

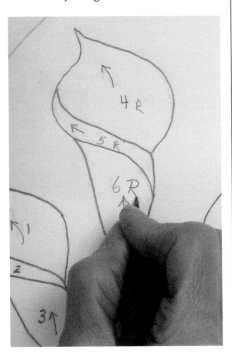

10. You now have a completed pattern for your project.

11. Remove the masking tape carefully and separate the papers.

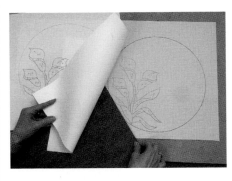

12. Use scissors to cut the tracing paper pattern into individual pattern pieces.

13. Your pattern in now ready for use in this project.

Projects

- [ ] Red and white streaky glass: $^1/_2$ square foot
- [ ] Fern green and white streaky glass: $^1/_2$ square foot
- [ ] $^1/_4$-inch thick clear glass: $11^1/_2$-inch circle
- [ ] Glass-cutting tools
- [ ] Pattern pieces
- [ ] Rubber cement
- [ ] Glass grinder
- [ ] Prepared photo fuse text decal (see page 92 for instructions for preparing the decal)
- [ ] Artist's brayer
- [ ] Shallow plate
- [ ] Distilled water
- [ ] Paper towels
- [ ] Prepared kiln shelf
- [ ] Thin kiln paper
- [ ] Prepared 12-inch round slumping mold

1. Glue each pattern piece onto the appropriate colored glass using rubber cement.

2. Follow your color grain arrows to position the pattern properly.

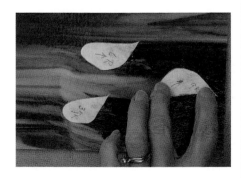

Pro Tip: Look for eye-catching color swirls and striations. These special markings are what will make your finished project unique and beautiful.

3. When all the pattern pieces have been glued into place, you will be ready to cut the glass.

4. Separate the glass into sections and cut out each individual piece of glass.

5. Continue cutting until all the pieces have been cut out.

Projects

99

6. Use a grinder to smooth the edges of each piece of glass.

7. Wash, rinse, and dry all glass pieces, including the clear base glass.

8. Place the 11½-inch circle of thick clear glass over the manila pattern. Position the design pieces of glass in their appropriate spaces according to the pattern.

9. Continue until all glass pieces are in place.

10. Carefully move the project onto a kiln shelf that has been covered with a piece of thin kiln paper.

11. Place the shelf and project into the kiln and check that no glass has shifted during the transfer from work table to kiln.

12. Use firing schedule B from page 34 or the firing guidelines below.

Firing Guidelines

Speed: Medium
Process: Contour Fuse
Top Temp: 1420°F
Hold Time: 12 Minutes

When the kiln has cooled to 100°F or less, you can remove your project.

13. Refer to the instructions on page 92 for preparing the Photo Fuse decal.

14. Trim the decal close to the text with scissors. You may need to separate the lines of text for better placement.

15. Place the decals face down in a shallow plate of distilled water.

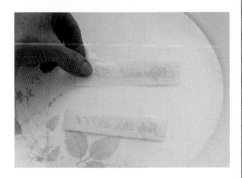

16. Soak the decals for about 90 seconds. Feel the edge of the decal to see if it is ready to slide off the protective backing.

17. Hold the left edge of the decal against the glass and slide the paper backing away.

18. Slide the decal into position on the glass. Repeat until all lines of text are in place.

19. Blot excess moisture with a paper towel.

20. Use a clean brayer to smooth the wrinkles from the decals.

21. Blot again with the paper towel to remove moisture and allow the decals to air-dry overnight.

22. Remove the kiln shelf from the kiln and position the round slumping mold over the kiln posts. Position your project over the mold and prepare to slump the glass.

23. Use firing schedule E from page 34 or the firing guidelines below.

Firing Guidelines

Speed: Slow
Process: Slump
Top Temp: 1250°F
Hold Time: 12 Minutes

24. After firing, allow the kiln to cool to 100°F or less before removing your project. Again, the photo fused decal has lightened to a sepia tone. Remove the glass from the mold and gently wash it to remove kiln paper and kiln wash residue.

With this project, you can see how incorporating some traditional stained glass cutting techniques with glass fusing creates a unique work of art.

In this project, we will break a picture into four separate tiles, and then reassemble them in a frame. Nearly any design could be used to make the tiles, so experiment with your favorite patterns. The pattern we used can be found on page 148.

- Separating a Design into Multiple Tiles
- Using Color Variations in Glass
- Using Bent Stringers

MATERIALS

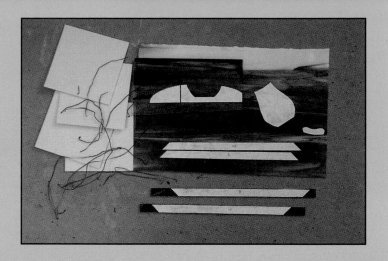

1. Cut four 4½-inch squares from the ivory opal glass. Cut four strips of the red opal glass, ½ inch wide.

2. Use scissors to cut out the pattern pieces for the borders, vase, and table.

3. Glue the table pattern onto the black and clear wispy glass with rubber cement. Look for a nice streak pattern to highlight.

4. Glue the vase pattern onto the red and white streaky glass. For our project, we chose to position the vase pattern diagonally across the color streaks and the lip of the vase horizontally.

Projects

103

5. Glue the pattern pieces for the border onto the red opal glass strips.

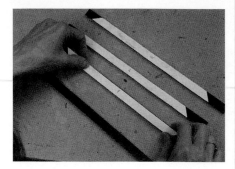

6. Cut the glass pieces according to the pattern.

7. Grind each piece carefully to smooth the edges of the glass.

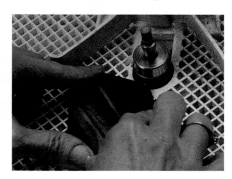

8. Check the fit of your glass pieces, especially where the vase fits into the table.

9. Wash, rinse, and dry all glass pieces.

10. On a prepared kiln shelf covered with a sheet of thin kiln paper, lay out the four ivory tiles, leaving about $3/8$ inch between the pieces. Add the border strips and the design pieces.

11. Begin arranging the bent stringers in an eye-catching design.

12. Break the stringers with your fingers where they cross from one tile to the next.

13. Continue adding stringers and breaking them where necessary.

A pair of tweezers can be helpful when adding small pieces.

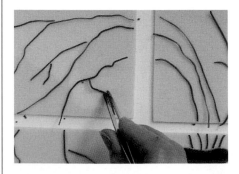

Your completed tiles should look something like this.

14. Use a clean brush to clean away any stringer particles from between the tiles.

15. A small spritz of hairspray will help to keep the stringers in place.

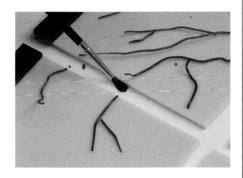

16. Carefully place the kiln shelf into the kiln.

17. Use firing schedule B from page 34 or the firing guidelines below.

Firing Guidelines

Speed: Medium
Process: Contour Fuse
Top Temp: 1400°F
Hold Time: 12 Minutes

18. When the kiln has cooled to 100°F or less, you can remove the tiles.

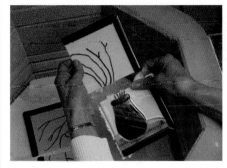

19. Wash away any residue from the kiln paper and dry the tiles thoroughly. The tiles are ready to glue into the wooden frame.

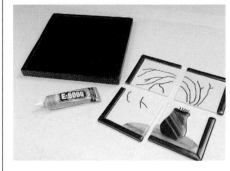

Apply the E6000 adhesive to the back of one tile, using a serpentine design.

20. Position the tile in the appropriate corner of the frame and press it gently into place.

21. Repeat for the remaining tiles and position them in their respective corners of the frame.

22. Place the frame on a flat surface and allow the adhesive to cure for 24 hours before moving.

This project can be displayed as a wall hanging or on a table.

Pendant lights have become very popular in the past few years. This iris light is not difficult to create and will look stunning in any room. The pattern can be found on page 149.

- Using Frit, Confetti, and Bent Stringers
- Draping Glass Over a Mold
- Drilling Through Glass with a Grinder
- Assembling a Pendant Light Fixture

Projects

MATERIALS

- [ ] Iridized clear glass with granite texture: 1 square foot
- [ ] Green and white streaky glass: ½ square foot
- [ ] Blue and white streaky glass: 1 square foot
- [ ] Godiva opal art glass: scrap
- [ ] Bent yellow opal stringers
- [ ] Bent blue stringers
- [ ] Cobalt blue medium frit
- [ ] Light blue fine frit
- [ ] Grape medium frit
- [ ] Grape fine frit
- [ ] Mardi Gras mini confetti
- [ ] Pattern
- [ ] Glass-cutting tools
- [ ] Grinder
- [ ] Prepared kiln shelf

- [ ] Thin kiln paper
- [ ] Tall floral former stainless steel mold
- [ ] Mold release
- [ ] Pendant light fixture
- [ ] Glass marker
- [ ] Ruler

1. Cut out four iris and leaf set designs according to the pattern. Grind the pieces, then wash, rinse, and dry the glass thoroughly.

2. Place the iridized clear granite glass on your work surface with the smooth side facing up. Lay out one iris/leaf motif in a corner of this glass.

3. Continue arranging the designs in each corner of the clear glass.

4. Break up the mini confetti pieces into even smaller bits and sprinkle over the design.

5. Add small pieces of the bent blue and yellow stringers between the flowers.

Projects

107

6. Mix together one spoonful of each type of frit in a small plastic cup.

Use a scoop to place the frit mixture above each iris.

7. When the project has been decorated to your satisfaction, place the glass on a prepared kiln shelf that has been covered with a sheet of thin kiln paper.

8. Carefully transfer the shelf to the kiln. Use firing schedule B from page 34 or the firing guidelines below.

Firing Guidelines

Speed: Medium
Process: Contour Fuse
Top Temp: 1400°F
Hold Time: 12 Minutes

9. When the kiln has cooled to 100°F or less, remove the glass from the kiln.

10. Prepare the tall floral former stainless steel mold by spraying it with an even coat of mold release.

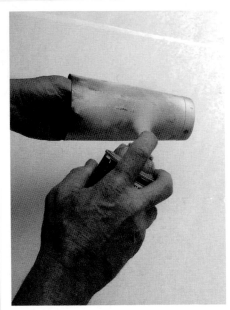

11. Determine the center of the glass by placing the ruler diagonally from corner to corner. Mark the midpoint with the glass marker.

12. Repeat this step in the opposite direction, and mark this midpoint with the glass marker. The center of the glass is the point where your markings intersect.

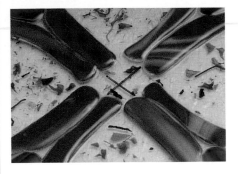

13. Mark the center of the closed end of the tall floral former with the glass marker.

14. Cover the prepared kiln shelf with a sheet of thin kiln paper. Center your floral former mold on the shelf.

Projects

15. Place the glass over the mold, matching the center of the glass with the center mark on the mold.

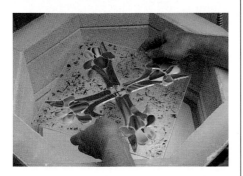

16. Remove the mark from the glass with a damp paper towel before firing.

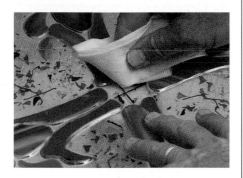

17. Use firing schedule E from page 34 or the firing guidelines below.

Firing Guidelines

Speed: Slow
Process: Slump
Top Temp: 1250°F
Hold Time: 12 Minutes

18. After cooling the kiln to 100°F or less, you can remove the slumped glass.

The project should slide freely from the stainless steel mold.

Notice the intricate folds that have formed as the glass slumped. Each piece fired over a floral former will have a different fold pattern.

Wash, rinse, and dry the glass.

ASSEMBLING THE PENDANT LIGHT

1. Remove the gasket from the light fixture to determine the size of the hole you will need to drill in the glass.

2. Center the gasket on the top of the slumped glass.

MATERIALS

- [ ] Grinder with a ¼-inch grinding head
- [ ] Wet sponge
- [ ] Fired iris glass
- [ ] Ruler
- [ ] Glass marker
- [ ] Safety glasses
- [ ] Pendant light fixture
- [ ] 40-watt lightbulb

3. Use the marker to trace the interior circle of the gasket onto the glass.

4. Hold the wet sponge against the ¼-inch grinder head. It is important to have the sponge in constant contact with the grinder head to keep the glass as cool as possible.

5. Turn the slumped glass over and center the marked circle on the grinder head. Do not use pressure, but allow the grinding surface to drill through the glass.

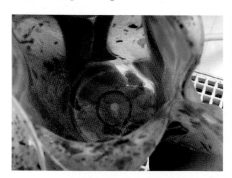

This picture shows the grinder head just as it has come through the glass.

6. By moving the glass in a circular motion, you can enlarge the opening up to your gasket marking.

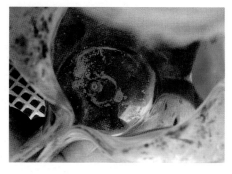

7. Check the fit of the light fixture. In this case, the opening is not quite large enough.

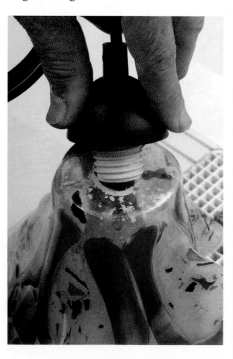

8. Continue grinding the interior of your marked circle until the light fixture will fit into the opening. Remember to keep the wet sponge against the grinder head during all grinding.

9. Clean the grinding debris away from the opening you have created.

10. Insert the light fixture through the opening and replace the gasket.

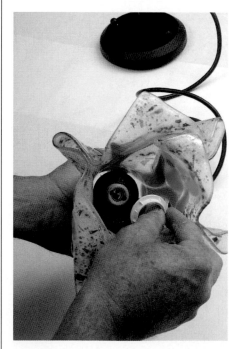

11. Add the lightbulb.

12. Check the light to make sure it is functioning properly before it is installed. Ah, yes! This pendant light is ready to hang.

Fiberboard is a great material for making your own molds. It is easy to cut with a putty knife or a paring knife and holds up well through many firings. For this project, I made a mold from Kaiser Lee Board, a popular brand of fiberboard. The vase will slump through the center opening of the mold.

The pattern can be found on page 150.

- • Using Fiber Board to Make a Drop Mold
- • Centering a Design
- • Slumping Glass Through a Drop Mold

MATERIALS FOR MAKING THE MOLD

- ☐ 8½-inch circle of Kaiser Lee fiber board
- ☐ Paper pattern
- ☐ Masking tape
- ☐ Pen
- ☐ Paring knife
- ☐ Dust mask
- ☐ Kiln wash
- ☐ Haik brush

MAKING THE MOLD

Note: Always wear a dust mask when working with fiberboard.

1. Begin by taping the pattern to the fiberboard circle with masking tape.

2. Trace the pattern design onto the fiberboard with a pen.

3. Use the paring knife to gently cut the design into the fiberboard. Don't try to cut through the entire thickness in one slice; you will find it more effective to work through a depth of ¼ to ½ inch at a time.

4. When you have completely cut through the fiberboard, carefully remove the center portion.

5. Use your fingers to lightly smooth the cut edges of the fiberboard mold.

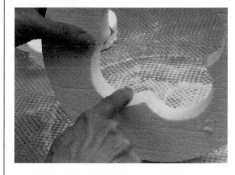

6. Smooth the top surface of the mold with your fingers.

7. Apply a coating of kiln wash over the mold with the Haik brush.

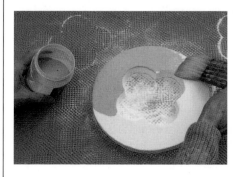

Projects

113

8. Make sure the kiln wash covers the interior cut edges of the mold.

9. The outer edges of the mold also need a coating of kiln wash.

10. Allow the kiln wash to air-dry thoroughly, and your mold will be ready to use. This material does not need to be prefired before using.

MAKING THE VASE

1. Use a fine point glass marker to trace the leaf templates on the green and white streaky glass. You will need four copies of each template.

MATERIALS FOR THE DROP VASE

☐ Iridized clear glass with a herringbone texture: 8⁷/₁₆-inch circle

☐ Sky blue glass: 8¹/₂-inch circle

☐ Dark green cathedral glass: scrap

☐ Fern green and white streaky glass: ¹/₂ square foot

☐ White opal glass: ¹/₄ square foot

☐ Fine-tipped glass marker

☐ Pattern templates

☐ Glass-cutting tools

☐ Grinder

☐ 4 small yellow opal nuggets

☐ Bent yellow opal stringers

☐ Hairspray (pump container)

☐ Thin kiln paper

☐ Prepared kiln shelf

☐ Three 3-inch kiln posts

2. Trace the flower petal template onto the white opal glass. You will need 25 flower petals.

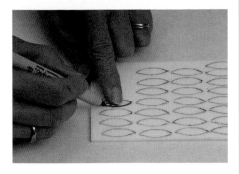

3. Use the stem template to trace four flower stems on the dark green cathedral glass.

4. Cut out all glass pieces.

5. Grind the glass to smooth the edges.

6. Wash, rinse, and dry all glass pieces.

7. Draw a large plus sign on a sheet of graph paper. This will help you in placing the design pieces symmetrically on the glass circles. Center the iridized clear circle over the plus sign with the herringbone texture facing up.

8. Position the sky blue circle evenly over the clear circle.

9. Begin to lay out the design by placing the first set of leaves and a stem on the glass. Use the upper line of the plus sign to guide the placement.

10. Continue placing leaves and stems until all four sets are in position.

11. Add six white flower petals around a yellow opal nugget center at the top of each stem. I like to use one extra flower petal in one of the flowers to honor the old saying, "He loves me, he loves me not."

Projects

115

12. You can use a wooden skewer or the handle of an artist's brush to help arrange the small glass pieces.

13. Some bent yellow opal stringers will add interest to your project. They look really neat when the vase is slumped.

14. A small spritz of hairspray will help hold the glass pieces in place.

15. Transfer the project from the work table to a prepared kiln shelf that has been covered with a sheet of thin kiln paper.

16. Carefully place the kiln shelf in the kiln, ready for the first firing.

17. Use firing schedule B from page 34 or use the firing guidelines below.

Firing Guidelines

Speed: Medium
Process: Contour Fuse
Top Temp: 1420°F
Hold Time: 12 Minutes

18. After the firing is complete, remember to allow the kiln to cool to 100°F or less before removing your glass.

19. You are now ready to set up the drop mold that you have made from the fiberboard. Place a fresh sheet of thin kiln paper on the prepared kiln shelf. Position the 3-inch kiln posts in a triangular arrangement.

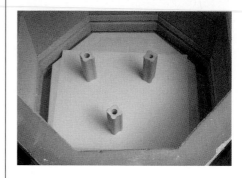

20. Place the fiberboard mold on top of the kiln posts. Make sure the posts are positioned near the outer edge of the mold so no glass will come in contact with the posts.

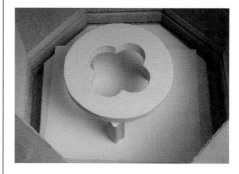

21. Center the fired project over the drop mold with the flowers positioned over the circular cutouts.

Projects

22. Your project is ready for the drop mold slumping.

Pro Tip: It is important to always check your project when the firing temperature nears the top temperature of the program. This is especially critical when firing a drop mold as the hold time at the top temperature can vary from one to three hours. Set a timer and check the progress of the drop every fifteen to twenty minutes during this hold time at the top temperature.

Use firing schedule F from page 34 or use the firing guidelines below.

Firing Guidelines

Speed: Slow
Process: Drop Slump
Top Temp: 1250°F
Hold Time: 60 to 180 Minutes

23. Remember to allow the kiln to cool to 100°F or less before removing the glass. Notice the texture trapped between the layers of glass from the herringbone design in the iridized clear glass. This is exactly the effect I was hoping to achieve.

24. Wash any residue of kiln wash or fiberboard from the glass. This project will look great in a wrought iron stand for display!

Note: When you check the progress of the slump, you will be looking to see that the glass has reached the kiln shelf. Allow the glass to flatten on the shelf, and begin the cooling process immediately. This floral vase completed its drop to the shelf in 180 minutes.

This sign incorporates many of the techniques shown in prior projects. It uses a photo-fusing decal, sifted powders, mixed frit, bent stringers, and small nuggets. It was designed with the assistance of Jayne Eckert. Using a variety of techniques will add interest to your projects. I chose to display my sign on a rustic barn board, but use your imagination to make your sign reflect your own distinctive style!

- Applying a Photo Fuse Text Decal
- Using Glass Powders and Frit
- Using Nuggets and Bent Stringers
- Attaching Glass to Wood

- [ ] Base glass: 8½ by 14-inch piece, with rough top edge if possible
- [ ] Fern green and white streaky glass: ½ square foot
- [ ] Dark amber cathedral glass: ½ square foot
- [ ] Light amber powder
- [ ] Dark green powder
- [ ] Scoop
- [ ] Powder sifter
- [ ] Dark green medium frit
- [ ] Dark purple medium frit
- [ ] Grape medium frit
- [ ] Light blue fine frit
- [ ] Small nuggets made from red, blue, and purple glass
- [ ] Bent stringers: dark green, purple, dark amber
- [ ] Tweezers
- [ ] Plastic mixing cup
- [ ] Pattern
- [ ] Scissors
- [ ] Glass-cutting tools
- [ ] Grinder
- [ ] Prepared photo-fuse decal

- [ ] Distilled water
- [ ] Shallow plate
- [ ] Clean artist's brayer
- [ ] Dry brush
- [ ] Wooden skewer
- [ ] Rustic wood for display
- [ ] E6000 adhesive
- [ ] Paper towels
- [ ] Hair spray (pump container)
- [ ] Prepared kiln shelf
- [ ] Thin kiln paper

Projects

1. Prepare your photo-fuse decal according to the instructions on page 92. Use scissors to trim the photo fuse decal close to the lettering. Place the decal face down in a shallow plate of distilled water.

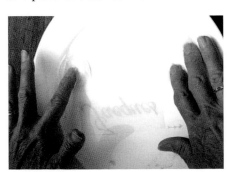

2. Soak the decal for 60 to 90 seconds and feel for the slip between the decal and the protective paper backing. When you feel the decal slipping, it is ready to slide onto the glass. Position the decal on your clean glass base.

3. Gently slide the paper backing from beneath the decal.

4. Check the spacing of your decal to make sure it is centered on your base glass.

5. Blot off excess moisture with a paper towel.

6. Smooth the decal onto the glass using a clean brayer. Blot again with a paper towel to remove moisture.

7. Use the scoop or a small spoon to put some light amber powder in the powder sifter.

Rub a pencil or brush handle over the ridged handle of the powder sifter to drift a fine layer of powder around the edges of your base glass.

8. Sift some dark green powder over the light amber powder in the same manner. Vary the amount of powder in some areas to produce an antique effect.

9. A small spritz of hairspray will keep the glass powders in place.

10. Cut the vines from the dark amber glass according to the pattern. There is no need to grind the edges of the glass, as you want the vines to look natural. Wash, rinse, and dry the vine pieces and place them on the base glass.

11. Use the nuggets to lay out a base layer for each of the grape clusters. Tweezers are an excellent tool for moving the nuggets into position.

12. Cut the leaves from the green and white streaky glass. A glass saw is very useful in cutting these intricate shapes. If a saw is not available for your use, split the leaf patterns into three sections for easier cutting. Grind any rough edges, then wash, rinse, and dry the leaves. Follow the pattern to place the leaves on your project, or use your sense of whimsy to arrange them in a pleasing design.

13. Add small sections of bent stringers for stems between each leaf and the grapevines.

14. Add a variety of bent stringer pieces to resemble tendrils coming off of the leaves and vines.

15. Use the scoop to add dark green medium frit around the leaves.

16. To add texture to your project, add some of the dark green frit on top of the leaves.

17. In the small plastic cup, mix together a spoonful of each shade of the blue and purple frit.

18. Use the scoop or a small spoon to place this frit mixture on the base glass and shape it to resemble small grape clusters.

19. A light mist of hairspray will help to hold your pieces in position.

20. Using tweezers, place a second layer of grapes over the larger grape clusters. This layer will not completely cover the first layer of grapes, but will cover some of the spaces between the individual grapes.

21. Allow the project to air-dry, and it will be ready for the kiln.

22. Place the project on a prepared kiln shelf that has been covered with a sheet of thin kiln paper. Use firing schedule A from page 34 or the firing guidelines below.

Use firing schedule A from page 34

Firing Guidelines

Speed: Medium
Process: Tack Fuse
Top Temp: 1375°F
Hold Time: 12 Minutes

23. When the kiln has cooled to 100°F or less, remove the glass and wash to remove any residue from the kiln wash. Dry thoroughly.

24. I have chosen an old barn board to display my sign on. The edges have been charred to give the wood a rustic appearance.

Turn the glass facedown and make a serpentine shape with the E6000 adhesive on the back of the project.

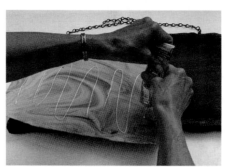

25. Position the glass in the center of the wood and lightly press into place.

26. This project should remain on a flat surface for at least 24 hours to allow the adhesive to set.

This wine cellar sign makes a great gift for your favorite wine connoisseur!

Projects

Reusing or recycling bottles by slumping them in the kiln is a lot of fun. Because we don't know the COE of a bottle, we can't add the glass to any other projects. However, there are many interesting ways to use the bottles once they have been flattened. Use your imagination to think up a new purpose for that old glass.

Before you put a bottle in the kiln, it should be washed and completely dry. Remove all paper and plastic labels. Painted labels can often withstand the heat of a firing, and a slumped bottle with this type of label makes an interesting conversation piece.

- Using Fusing Wire
- Flattening Bottles in a Kiln
- Slumping Flattened Bottles into a Mold

- [ ] Wire cutters
- [ ] Needle-nose pliers
- [ ] 17-gauge fusing wire
- [ ] Various bottles—clean and completely dry
- [ ] Thin kiln paper
- [ ] Prepared kiln shelf

1. To make a hook for a wine bottle, cut a 2½-inch length of the 17-gauge fusing wire with the wire cutters. (For smaller bottles, use 24-gauge fusing wire, cut to a length of 1½ inches.) Use needle-nose pliers to bend the ends of the wire inward.

2. Fold the hook in half over the handle of your pliers.

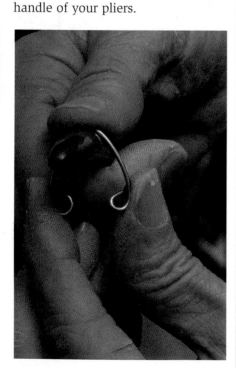

Your finished hook should look similar to this.

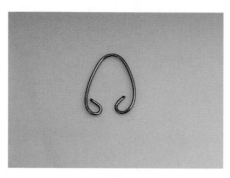

3. Insert the hook in the mouth of the bottle.

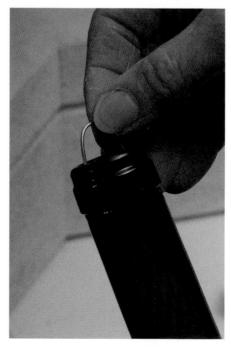

4. Place the wine bottles on a prepared kiln shelf covered with a sheet of thin kiln paper. Allow a 3- to 4-inch space between the bottles.

5. Use firing schedule D from page 34 or the firing guidelines below.

Firing Guidelines

Speed: Slow
Process: Full Fuse
Top Temp: 1480°F
Hold Time: 20 Minutes

6. Cool the kiln to 100°F or less before removing the bottles from the kiln.

Projects

7. There are several styles of slumping molds that you can use to change the shapes of your flattened bottles. Here, we have removed the kiln shelf and placed the slumping mold directly on the kiln posts.

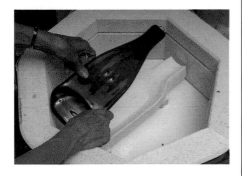

8. Center the bottle over the slumping mold and fire to a slump temperature.

9. Use firing schedule E from page 34 or the firing guidelines below.

Firing Guidelines

Speed: Slow
Process: Slump
Top Temp: 1250°F
Hold Time: 12 Minutes

Allow the kiln to cool to 100°F or less before removing the glass from the kiln.

Here are a few unique examples of flattened bottles.

Flattened bottles with painted labels.

Embossed bottles by Tina Harris.

Photo fused bottle with stencil.

Etched bottles. Designs by Betsy Gibbs.

Small bottle wind chime with etching.

The Lemonade Bowl

A regular customer of Rainbow Vision Stained Glass likes to cite the old adage that when life hands you lemons, you make lemonade. That sage advice led me to try something new and innovative.

One day, some shoppers had pulled a piece of confetti and streamer glass off the shelf to admire its beauty. They put the sheet of glass back on the shelf and had moved to the opposite end of the glass rack when the confetti and streamer glass fell to the floor and shattered. I swept the shards into the dustpan but couldn't bear to throw them away; there had to be some way to use this lovely glass. The dustpan of glass sat at the back of the work table for months.

Finally, I decided to see if the shards could be reassembled. Slowly, I put the glass back together again.

Only a few tiny pieces were missing. Using the technique shared by Spectrum Glass Company for their Crack-Up Platter, I rebuilt the glass pieces on a base sheet of mauve cathedral glass. As the Spectrum instructions advised, I left space between the pieces to allow for more definition.

The glass was fired to a contour fuse at 1420°F, and then slumped into a mold.

Instead of a dustpan full of broken glass to be thrown away, I have an interesting bowl with a unique story behind it. So if a project doesn't turn out the way you had anticipated, don't look at it as a failed piece. Make some lemonade!

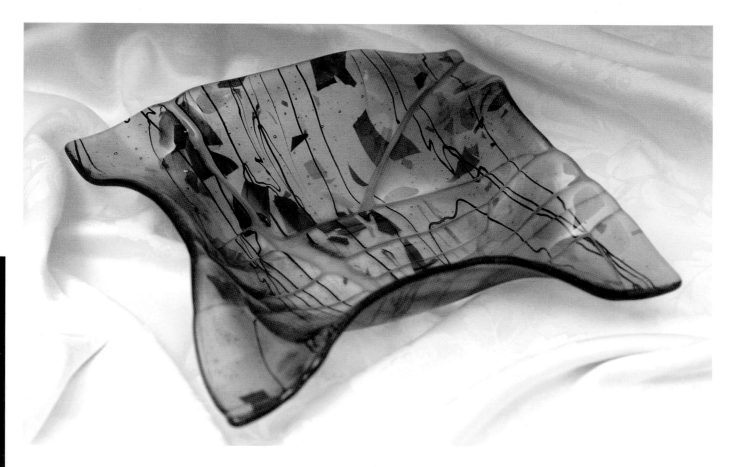

Gallery

This section showcases the art of colleagues and fusing students. We hope their work is an inspiration to you as you explore your own creativity.

Sun-Face Patio Table by Tina Harris. Based on a design by Dione Roberts in *Mosaic Stepping Stones,* published by CKE Publications, Olympia, Washington.

Chili Peppers Windchime by Lee Summers.
Original design.

Wildlife Collage Panel by Tess Gray. Original design.

Radiant Sun Bird Bath by Lynn Haunstein. Based on a design by Mari Stein in *The Sun, The Moon, and the Stars,* published by Marick Studios, Cincinnati, Ohio.

Iris Candleholder by Lee Summers. Iris based on a design by Debra and Steven Van Tol in *Sun-Sculptures I,* published by Village Glass Works, Auburn, Michigan.

129

Logo for the Pennsylvania Statewide Adoption
Network, fabricated by Michael Johnston.

Dragonfly Window Tile by Sarah Riling.
Original design.

Photo-fused Tree of Life Wall Hanging by Denise Hackman.

Lilies by Nan Maund. Based on a design by Patrice Lampton in *A Touch of Tiffany*, published by CKE Publications, Olympia, Washington.

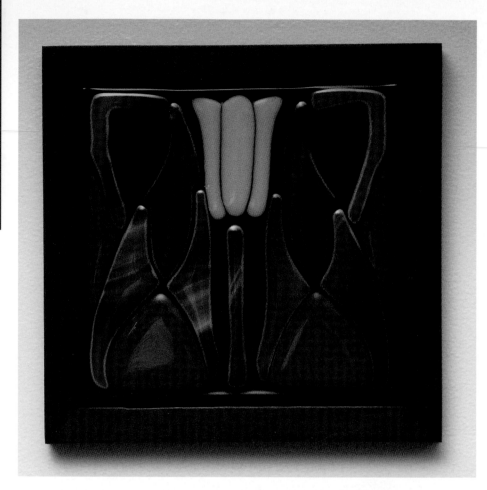

Lotus Tile by Lee Summers. Based on a design by Motawi Tileworks, published in *Cottages and Bungalows,* published by Beckett Media, LLC, Anaheim, California.

Pink Dichroic Earrings and Pendant by Lynn Cornelius. Original design.

Heart Pendant by Lynn Cornelius. Original design.

Black and Silver Dichroic Earrings and Pendant by Lynn Cornelius. Original design.

Drop Vases by Lynn Haunstein. Original designs.

Aquarium by Janet McKelvey. Original design.

Autumn Leaves Candle Holder by Michael Johnston. Original design.

Falling Stars Votive Cup by Nan Maund. Original design.

Sushi Plate by Michele Zelonis. Original design.

Sushi Plate and Wasabi Dish by Denise Hackman. Original design.

Swiss Cheese Plate by Tina Harris.
Based on a demonstration video at
www.bisqueimports.com.

Walking on Water Plate by Betsy Gibbs. Original design.

Origami Bowl by Michele Zelonis. Original design.

Christmas Plates by Tess Gray. Original designs.

Pisces Bowl by Betsy Gibbs. Based on a design by Robert Oddy, published in *Glass Patterns Quarterly*, Westport, Kentucky.

Cat on a Crescent Moon Plate by Lynn Haunstein. Original design.

Acknowledgments

Many people have been instrumental in making this book possible and seeing it through to its completion. Their roles and talents deserve special recognition.

First, I wish to thank Mark Allison and Kathryn Fulton of Stackpole Books for the opportunity to write *Basic Glass Fusing*. They have been most helpful with their guidance.

I am grateful to Alan Wycheck for his beautiful photography. It is through his trained eyes that you are seeing glass and fusing projects to their best advantage. Thanks, Alan.

Very special thanks to my colleagues at Rainbow Vision Stained Glass in Harrisburg, Pennsylvania. To Michael Johnston, my mentor and sounding board, my sincere gratitude. It was your spark of an idea that grew into this book. To my friends and coworkers, Jan McKelvey, Nan Maund, and Lee Summers: You are just the best people to work with and I appreciate your support. And to our fusing students, thanks for asking the questions that help us all learn more about this art form. You keep me on my toes!

Last, but never the least, my deepest gratitude to my family. To Jim, this book is for you. Your love and care over the past 38 years have never wavered. Thank you for the chance to explore my passion for glass. To our daughters, Jennifer, Katie, and Elizabeth, I offer my appreciation for your interest and support. Thanks for accepting the good as well as the not-so-good project gifts. And Katie, your expertise in proofreading and formatting were especially helpful. *Muchas gracias y buena suerte!*

Patterns

In this section, you will find the patterns for the projects in this book. Once you are comfortable working with fused glass, I encourage you take the processes described and use your own creative spirit to apply them to your own original designs.

Orchid Garden Stake

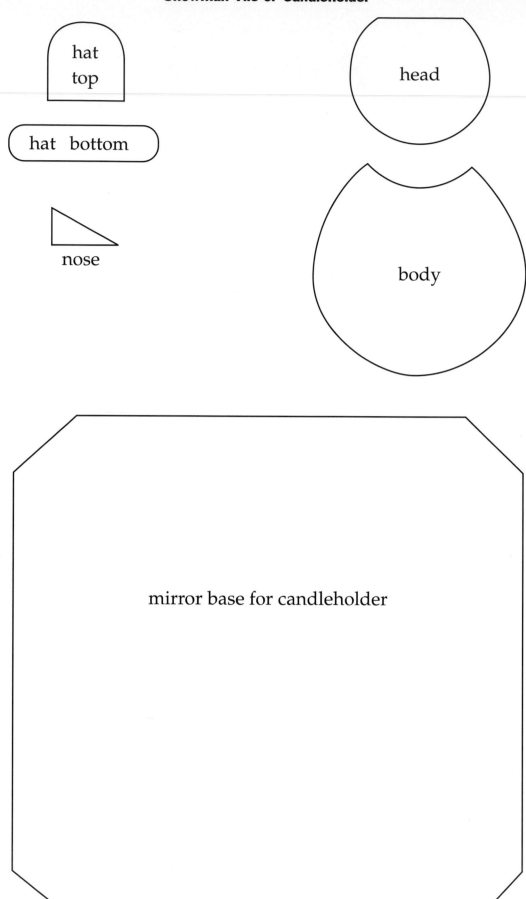

hat
top

hat bottom

nose

head

body

mirror base for candleholder

Christmas Tree Windchime

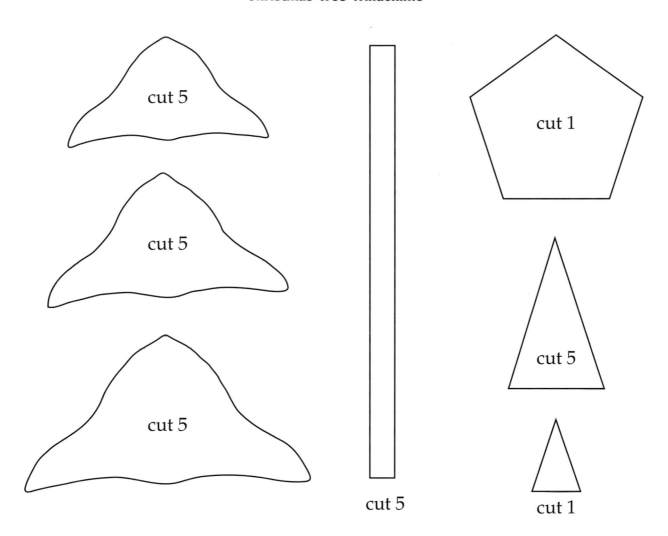

cut 5

cut 5

cut 5

cut 5

cut 1

cut 5

cut 1

Embossed Easter Ornaments

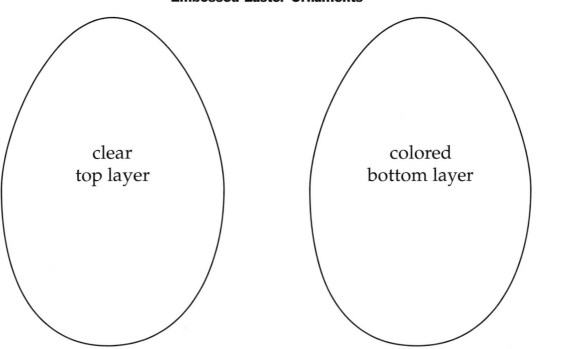

clear
top layer

colored
bottom layer

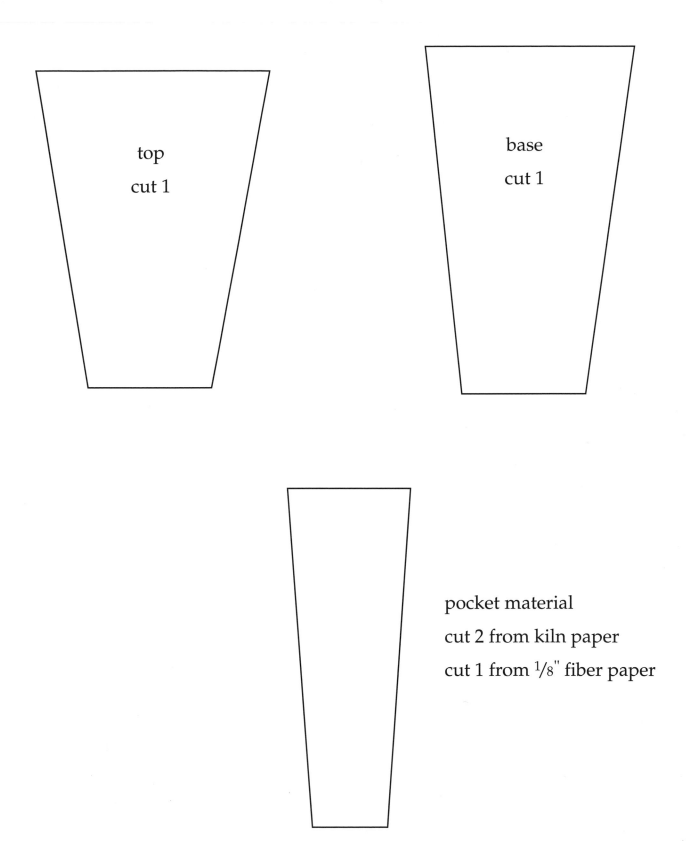

top

cut 1

base

cut 1

pocket material

cut 2 from kiln paper

cut 1 from $1/8"$ fiber paper

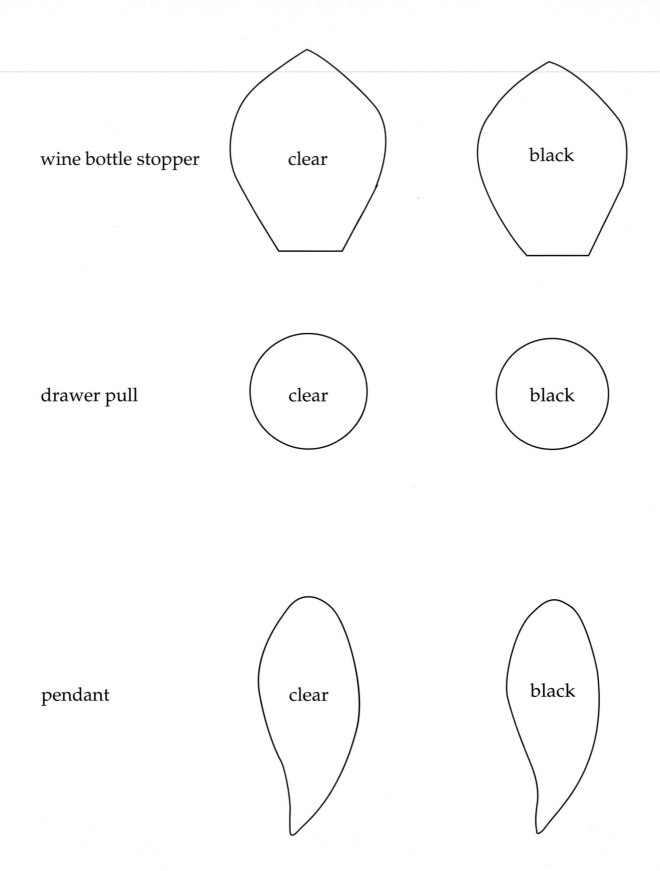

wine bottle stopper

clear

black

drawer pull

clear

black

pendant

clear

black

Framed Tile Picture

cut 4

border pieces

cut 4

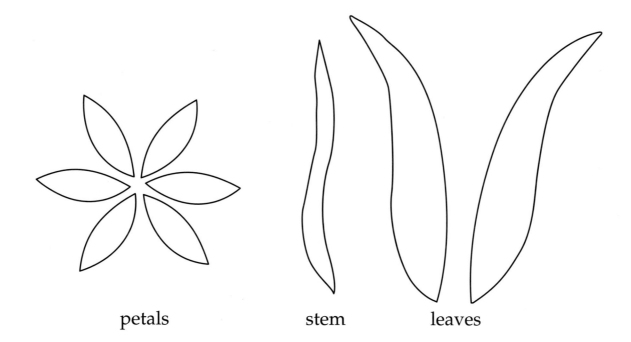

petals   stem   leaves

cut 24 white petals

cut 4 green stems

cut 4 green left leaves

cut 4 green right leaves

mold pattern

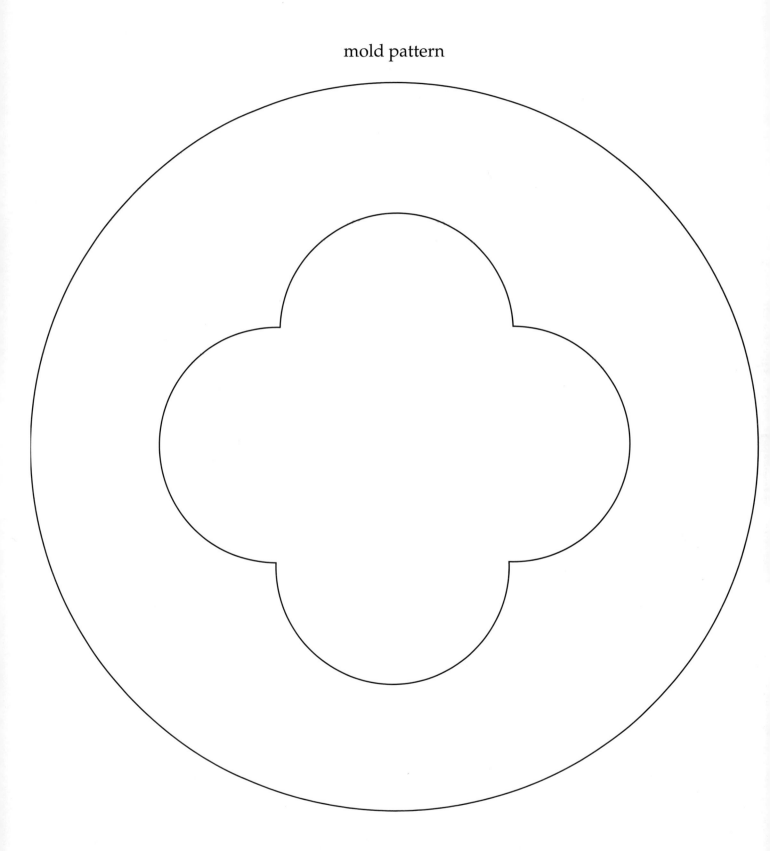

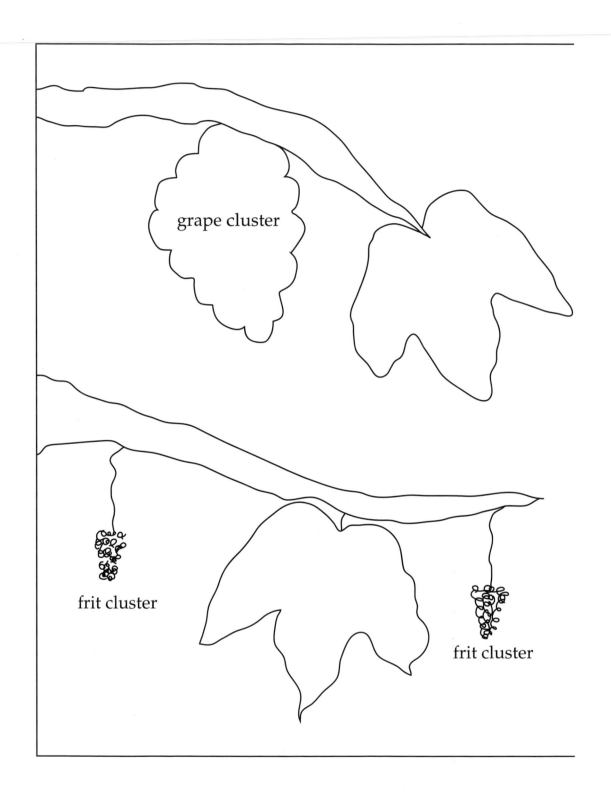

grape cluster

frit cluster

frit cluster

grape cluster

frit cluster

grape cluster

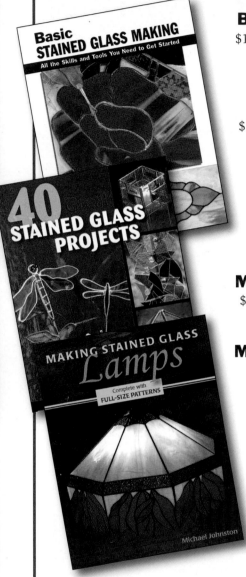